**A
PUBLIC
SPACE
No. 32**

When we alter a component of our perceptions, what becomes of us in not seeking readjustment?
—Brigid Hughes

Cildo Meireles

No. 32

TABLE OF CONTENTS

02 — *The Editor*

03 — *project*
Insertions into Ideological Circuits
CILDO MEIRELES

08 — *fiction*
A Short Tractate on Fine Art
YORDANKA BELEVA
TRANSLATED BY IZIDORA ANGEL
He taught us to believe in the imaginary but never to seek it because if we were to find it, a yearning would die away.

10 — *survey*
Atlantic City
JACK BOUCHER

12 — *poetry*
Voyage
JAMES SHEA
Cameos of the unknown.

14 — *jewelry*
ART SMITH

16 — *fiction*
The Desert
NAZ RIAHI
I tried to meet the tenderness of her offering with my own gentleness, which never came easy.

29 — *oral history*
The Chimney Girl
PETER TRACHTENBERG
The past looks different when viewed in the glare of the future.

36 — *fiction*
Accidents
ANNA BALLBONA
TRANSLATED BY LAWRENCE VENUTI
The amazing thing is how precise the result of an accident can be.

42 — *art*
KATE SHEPHERD

44 — *fiction*
Astraea
KATE KRUIMINK
She needed to scrape her mind clean like a farrier scraping a horse's hoof.

96 — *poetry*
SUZANNE BUFFAM
KIRSTEN KASCHOCK
MIKE LALA
GRAHAM FOUST

102 — *essay*
Eye and Mind
CALVIN GIMPELEVICH
How many more deserving things have I forgotten, while the image of the sun and woman remains?

111 — *fiction*
Suboptimal
MEGAN CUMMINS
She'd wanted to laugh from the beginning.

124 — *art*
ROSEMARY LAING

126 — *poetry*
KIMIKO HAHN
ADAM CLAY
SAMIRA NEGROUCHE
TRANSLATED BY NANCY NAOMI CARLSON

132 *fiction*

Skin Fades
MATEO ASKARIPOUR
Vengeance didn't dwell in him..

150 *stories out of school*

Lockdown Drill
ANNE P. BEATTY
"Why's it there?" she whispers.

152 *portraits*

Jump
PHILIPPE HALSMAN

154 *fiction*

Where Are You and Where Is My Money?
UCHEOMA ONWUTUEBE
I do not write to make trouble.

172 *poetry*

Portraits of My Aunt on Her Sickbed
YEE HENG YEH
Enough of fiction and its diminutions.

177 *fiction*

The Cove
CJ GREEN
He seemed to be smiling at the memory, as if he too were bidding a private farewell to the person he had been.

193 *journey*

Erosion
CORY HOWELL HAMADA
I had a strange sense of comfort, as if pausing for a moment of peace after navigating to the center of a labyrinth

204

Notes on Contributors .

Perhaps this is why I feel the need to put all these scenes in order. It's as if in stacking up these lines, one on top of the other, I align my universe a little. —Anna Ballbona

A PUBLIC SPACE
(ISSN 1558-965X;
ISBN 9781736370940)
IS PUBLISHED BY
A PUBLIC SPACE
LITERARY PROJECTS, INC.
PO BOX B
NEW YORK, NY 10159.
PRINTED IN THE US.
ISSUE 32, ©2024
A PUBLIC SPACE
LITERARY PROJECTS, INC.
POSTMASTER PLEASE
SEND CHANGES OF
ADDRESS TO A PUBLIC
SPACE, PO BOX B, NEW
YORK, NY 10159.

**A PUBLIC SPACE
IS SUPPORTED
IN PART BY**

**A PUBLIC SPACE IS A
PROUD MEMBER OF**
The Community of
Literary Magazines and
Presses

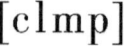
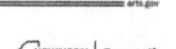

No. 32 **A PUBLIC SPACE**

EDITOR
Brigid Hughes

PROGRAMS MANAGER
Aditi Bhattacharjee

COMMUNICATIONS DIRECTOR AND EDITORIAL ASSOCIATE
Alexandra Tilden

EDITORIAL FELLOWS
Lydia Mathis
Louis Harnett O'Meara
Maurice Rodriguez

ASSOCIATE EDITORS
Sarah Blakley-Cartwright
Sidik Fofana
Taylor Michael

ASSISTANT EDITOR
Miguel Coronado

SENIOR COPY EDITOR
Anne McPeak

READERS
Hristo Karastoyanov
Maria Catalina Heitmann
Meagan Washington

INTERN
Klein Voorhees

CONTRIBUTING EDITORS
Annie Coggan
Martha Cooley
Edwin Frank
Mark Hage
John Haskell
Yiyun Li
Fiona Maazel
Ayana Mathis
Robert Sullivan
Antoine Wilson

POETRY EDITOR
Brett Fletcher Lauer

COVER DESIGN
Janet Hansen

PUBLICITY
Kait Astrella

INTERNATIONAL CONTRIBUTING EDITORS
Dorthe Nors (Denmark)
Natasha Randall (England)
Motoyuki Shibata (Japan)

EDITORS AT LARGE
Megan Cummins
Elizabeth Gaffney

BOARD OF DIRECTORS
Katherine Bell
Charles Buice
Rimjhim Dey
Elizabeth Gaffney
Brigid Hughes
Yiyun Li
Robert Sullivan

ADVISORY BOARD
Robert Casper
Fiona McCrae
James Meader

FOUNDING BENEFACTOR
Deborah Pease
(1943-2014)

SUBSCRIPTIONS
Postpaid subscription for 3 issues: $36 in the United States; $54 in Canada; $66 internationally. Subscribe at www.apublicspace.org or send a check to the address below.

CONTACT
For general queries, please email general@apublicspace.org or call (718) 858-8067. A Public Space is located at PO Box B New York, NY 10159.

FICTION / YORDANKA BELEVA / TRANSLATED FROM THE BULGARIAN BY IZIDORA ANGEL

A SHORT TRACTATE ON FINE ART

He taught us to believe in the imaginary but never to seek it because if we were to find it, a yearning would die away. And he was the father of all our yearnings—our fine art teacher.

He was gentle with our first efforts. *Paint every time you cry. Paint as though you're about to cry. A watercolor is a landscape seen through tears. Put on your grandfather's glasses, stand behind the steamed-up windows of a train receding into the distance. Only when you recede into the distance can you appreciate just how close you are to the scenery.*

Until the end of his life he remained attached to something that was always missing. To someone whose portrait was eternally paling. To him pale and flesh-toned were synonymous, or the same person, because it was only in the wan, foggy mornings that he fleetingly detected what he'd lost. But when the fog dissipated, we saw clearly the contours of a melancholy man.

He carried his sorrow around like a tripod, the three legs sharp as blades, like the three points of breathing. And the pierced air bled a new hue every time. He painted but never showed his paintings. We hypothesized what they may have depicted based on that day's assignment.

Split your canvas in two. On the left, paint your happiest day, on the right, your unhappiest. As homework, paint the line you put between the two days as the interior of a house.

He gave all our houses perfect scores. Regardless of whether they were overly busy and colorful or multistoried and structurally impossible, he marked every last one as excellent. The other teachers reminded him this was not sustainable or didactic, that he was cutting off our limbs, maiming our criteria for what was proper and aesthetic. *Who am I to edit a child's view of the world,* he defended himself.

His refusal to dictate the direction of the human gaze was the most permanent belief in his world: Something like the child he could have had and raised in a house just like other people did. *Just like* is the death of all art, he said. He'd saved himself on numerous occasions—he could have had a studio *just like*, fame *just like*, muses *just like*. He allowed himself what ifs only with colors and preconceptions.

He often had us over to his home. *Come here anytime.* Some of us went for confirmation that the house was empty, others went and saw in the emptiness the space to finish a painting. He worked more with the second group. He domesticated them for the wild.

Once, he split our class in two. Thematically. One half was to paint the perfect life, the other—man's best friend. He wanted us to *see* whether there would be a difference. As he helped us discover it, he calibrated our senses to feel that *everything is all the same, it matters only who is holding the brush*.

Here we are now, cleaving all of sorrow. Not all of us, his disciples, are here; but couldn't any one of us contain this universal loss. Our fine art teacher lies in a coffin. Some kind of thrown together, absurd final portrait. A charcoal painting in candlelight. That's one he didn't show us in school. I'd never considered a coffin as an easel before. People walk up, they lean over, then each person paints according to the saturation of his individual loss. The collective canvas of farewell. After it's framed, the painting is lowered into storage, but the exhibition continues. It will last as long as there is someone to talk about it.

Our life began with cave drawings and it'll end inside a painting of a prefab Soviet block, our teacher liked to joke.

He taught us well: *Everything, every last fragment, is on par with the whole.*

Something like gathering carnations and candles into a nature morte painting above a portrait of deeply shut eyes amid a landscape of forlorn faces.

The small in scale, well placed, does present a problem for the expansionist; size and might become mired in the apportioning of sympathies. In defending the diminutive, one sees in us the needs of the wide-eyed newborn.

Jack Boucher

VOYAGE

JAMES SHEA

Whenever I watch a black-and-white film

I think of how all the extras are dead,

I don't think about the stars this way,

they are larger than life on the screen,

shown in close-up, best lit, the film

a testament to their afterlife, but those

extras sadden me with their walk-ons,

cameos of the unknown, they still exist

in some manner here before me, but

in the brevity of their appearance

they are vigorously alive and gone—

a vitality at doing nothing in particular,

not drawing too much attention, quickly

cast aside, that's who I am off camera,

were the director to pan suddenly to me

on my couch—missed more than the stars,

for they have no lines, no special directions,

just told to act naturally without words.

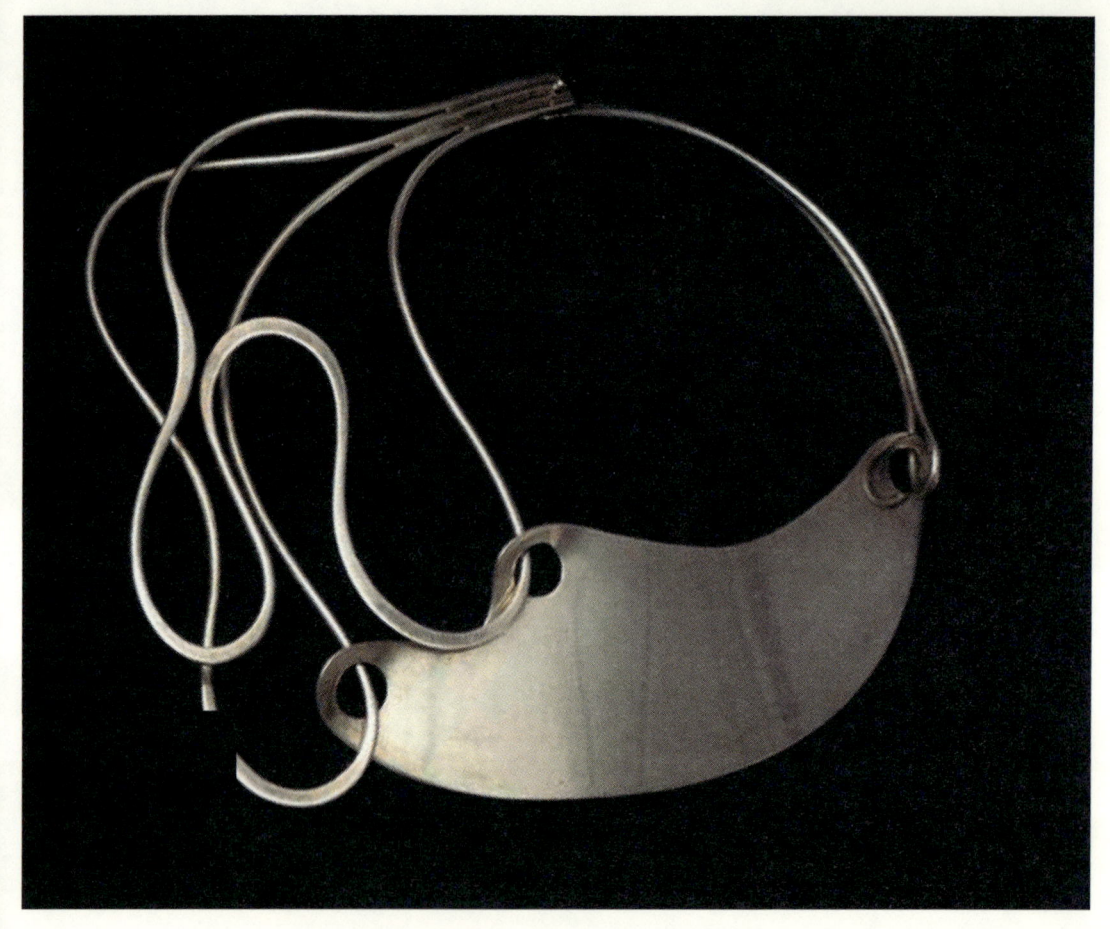

The rigid link does not create the perfect curve of the chain and the catenary

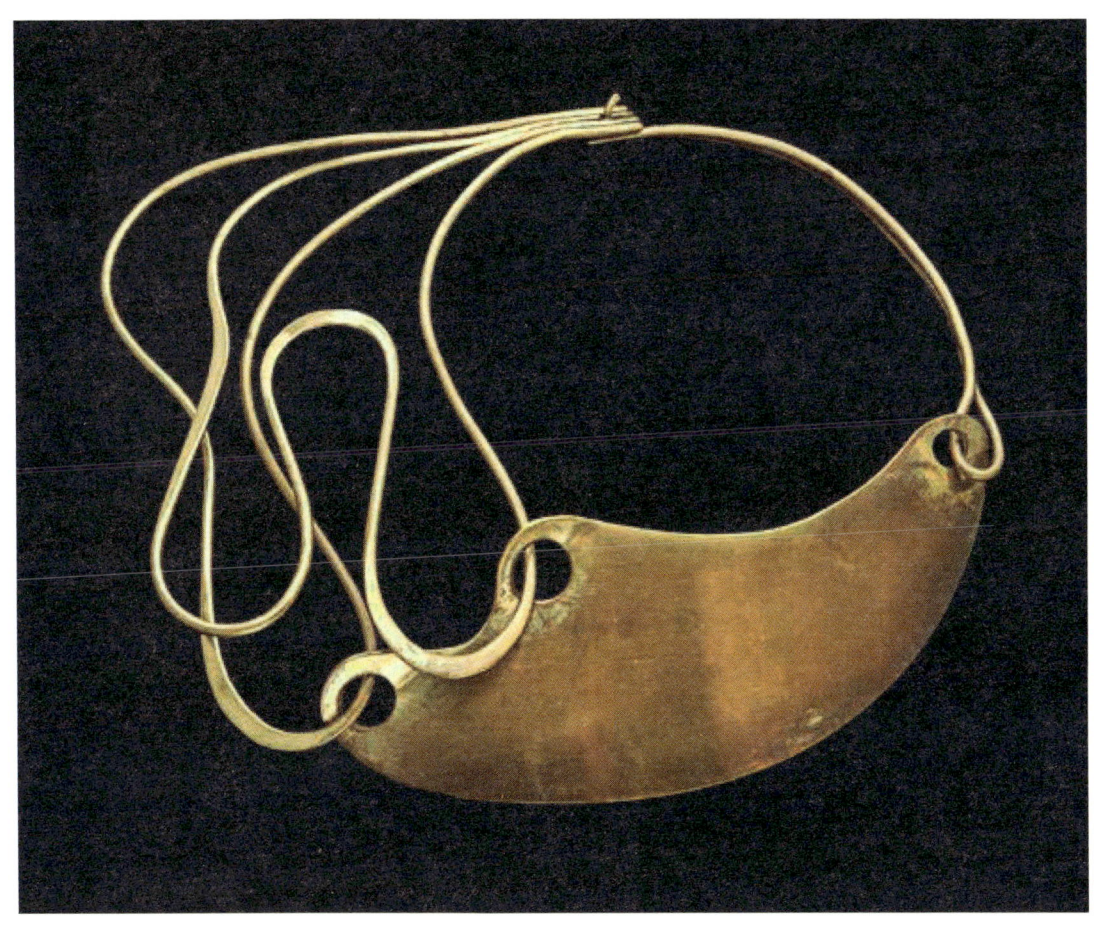

but in approximating, it pulls away from nature's demand for ubiquity.

Art Smith

FICTION

THE DESERT
NAZ RIAHI

"Why is she smiling?" I asked.

A toddler was stumbling toward us, in the drunken way they do.

"She thinks she's very cute," my mother replied. We were speaking Farsi.

"She looks old," I said. "Like an old lady."

My mother smiled at the baby, and the effort was visible as she waved.

I looked back at the girl. She waved.

Her mother—a strikingly Scandinavian-looking woman,

very tall and with long, straight blond hair—trailed behind. Her father was also tall, but dark haired and olive skinned. He sat at a nearby table with his phone.

"I hope she's not bothering you," the mother said to us.

"She's adorable," my mother said, in her thickly accented English.

"Thank you. I give her a lot of room to figure things out. I'm not sure if that's a good or a bad way to parent."

My mother had always said she wanted to take a trip to Italy with me. She wanted us to go to Rome and Venice. She wanted to see Florence again, where she'd been with my father on their honeymoon. There are photos of her back then, at twenty, her hair long and radiant, the subject of his love and lens.

I wanted to give her this trip to Italy badly, but it was never the right time and I never had enough money to do it the way I wanted. Two nights in the desert at the Parker Palm Springs, on my credit card points, was the best I could do.

In the car from Los Angeles we'd both complained about how much we disliked children at hotels, especially expensive ones.

"I don't understand why parents have to take their children everywhere with them in America," she said. We'd been living here for almost thirty years, but America was still foreign to her. She didn't understand the culture, its intentions. She thought Americans were loud, showered too much, weren't well-read.

"American women all look like wet cats, going to work in the morning with their wet hair," she'd say. Or, "Why do the children in this country need so many snacks?"

I often wondered if she'd be able to live in Iran again. I asked myself the same question—would I be able to live there again?—even though I'd come in childhood and she in her forties.

"We just left the kids at home and asked the neighbor to check in on them," she said.

"You took me everywhere with you," I said.

"I had no choice. But these people, they have choices."

"I was your accessory. You showed me off."

"Yes," she said, as if that were all there was to parenting.

The drive east had been awful. I'd picked her up at Union Station, but she hadn't been able to find the right exit, and there were panicked calls about homeless people. I should have parked and gone in to meet her train, but I was late and I worried about traffic. She should have said, You should have parked. But she didn't, and that somehow made it worse.

It took us a while to get comfortable with each other again. That was always the case. This was our first trip together alone, as adults. The last time we'd traveled together was nearly thirty years before, when we'd escaped Iran.

We'd flown from Tehran to Istanbul, and checked into a hotel with a marble lobby that went all the way up to the sky. The hotel's clean, modern lines were a world away from anything I'd seen in Tehran. It was beautiful and safe. I could breathe. The hotel had a pool, and each night I dove in with my eyes closed, as if the water could cleanse my grief and everything that had happened at home before we left. My mother, uninterested in the pool, disappeared into the hotel's shops.

During the few days we stayed in Istanbul, she and I walked around the city together. I kept my eyes peeled for the playground my father had taken me to the last time we'd visited Turkey. Before he was executed. I didn't know then that all of Turkey wasn't Istanbul, that the playground with its steep slide that frightened and thrilled me, and the memory, one of very few I had of my father, was three hundred miles away in Izmir.

From Istanbul, my mother and I flew to Vienna. Our ultimate destination was Hawaii. My mother had never been there but she had seen pictures and believed Hawaii to be a paradise in America. She told me that she and my father had talked about settling there if they could get out of Iran and figure out how to make a living in this country.

In Vienna we checked into a tiny, centuries-old pension owned by an Iranian couple that friends of my mother had known. Gone were the tall ceilings and bright rooms of our Istanbul hotel. I hated the heavy curtains and maroon carpeting. I hated Vienna with its soot-covered architecture, the devastating quaintness of our hotel, and all the old people in the dining room, eating dinner while it was still light out.

From our hotel room, my mother was busy planning our life in America, jotting notes and using a phone card to call an old friend in Oahu. I was sad and bored. She got me a camera to distract me. My father had a Nikon that he loved almost as much as he loved us. It was one of the few things of his I'd asked if I could have—the camera along with his watch and dog tags. But I hadn't yet dared to use it. I didn't even know how.

My father was the chronicler of our tiny family—hardly in any photos himself. Once on a holiday to the Caspian Sea, I snuck inside the house where we were staying, while everyone was at the beach, to play with his camera. I must have been six. I didn't know how to use it, so I pressed button after button until the back of the camera flung open, exposing the film just as my father walked in and flew into a rage. It was the most wonderful thing I'd ever held in my hands.

The camera my mother gave me was a point and shoot. She showed me how to load the film and told me I could go down to the lobby to take pictures, which I did with fervor. Over the course of our time in Vienna I took three rolls of photos: lopsided images of furniture, blurry ones of people, unmoored photos of clouds, photos of flamingos at the zoo where my mother and I spent one afternoon. And a photo I secretly snapped of two leather-and-spike-clad punks kissing on the street. I'd never seen a teenage boy and girl like that. I worried that if my mother saw me looking at them she'd make me look away.

My favorite photo was a close up of the woman who owned the pension. My mother had said to me, "I bet she can sing. Her top teeth protrude out over her bottom teeth."

After a few days of working up my courage, I'd gone down and asked her if she could sing for me.

"Sing for you?" she said.

"My mom says you have a nice voice."

"How does she know that?" she said.

"Your top teeth are big," I said.

She covered her mouth and giggled.

"What's your favorite song?" she said.

"'Mara Beboos,'" I said. A song about leaving.

She began to sing, and as she did I raised my camera and clicked the shutter open and closed. In the picture, the lower half of her face, her open mouth, are in focus while the upper half tilts back, blurring into the dark background of the front desk.

After lunch my mother and I went to the spa where I'd booked us massages. We sat by the indoor salt pool. My mother took off her caftan to reveal a body

I didn't recognize. In her one-piece swimsuit I could see that her shape had morphed. Where once she was slender and toned, she'd developed a fleshy mass. Her thighs were gently pock marked with cellulite, and from her bikini line, a sliver of gray hair was exposed.

She saw me looking. "I've gained so much weight," she said.

The body I remembered seemed to have belonged to another woman, meticulously looked after, groomed. I took off my clothes, a little self-conscious now, and laid down with my book, the letters between Audre Lorde and Pat Parker. My mother took out her tablet to play poker.

I don't think I'd grasped, until that moment, my own changing body. The way my belly had filled in and was softer, the broadening of my feet as I'd grown out of my high-heel habit and settled into Birkenstocks and sneakers. An aesthetic choice that inadvertently became irreversible.

There was so much I'd admired about my mother's beauty as a little girl. And there was so much about the reality of her decay that I feared.

"I love that book," a woman on a lounge chair a few feet away said.

"I don't know anyone else who's read it," I said.

"I take it you're a fan?" she said.

"Very much a fan of Lorde, but to be honest I was unfamiliar with Pat Parker's work until this."

The woman, in her forties with a short haircut that was at once boyish and sexy, came to sit on the lounge chair right next to me.

"I've always wanted that," she said.

"A pen pal?"

She laughed.

"I had one of those in fourth grade. I've always wanted the mentorship. The camaraderie. They were sisters in arms."

"And it was all documented."

"Exactly!" she said. "There's such romance to it."

"To their friendship?"

"In the way they opened themselves to each other. In the way they hurt each other and protected each other from the world."

Her name was Darla and she was a designer, in the desert for Design Week, which I'd known about but hadn't had the inclination to attend. My mother wasn't one for sightseeing or museums. It was the mall or the pool or just plain home for her.

"What did she want?" my mother asked when Darla went back to her chair.

Though she spoke English well enough, when I was around she relied on me to translate.

"She was asking about my book," I said.

Soon our massage therapists came and for ninety minutes we each went our separate ways. Afterward I saw her in the locker room getting dressed.

"Do you want to get in the sauna before we go?"

"Will it take a long time?"

"Where do you have to be?"

At this, she laughed.

In the sauna she wore her swimsuit and sat on a towel she'd neatly folded. I went in naked, having learned this from the Korean women at my gym.

"I always wanted to see you naked," she said. "When you were young and your body was changing. But you wouldn't let me. I thought it was so cruel."

"I hated it," I said. "I hated how my body changed. I don't think I'll ever grow accustomed to any of these changes."

"I know. I hated it, too. It was unfair."

"That I wouldn't take my clothes off in front of you?"

"For a long time you had belonged to me, you were a piece of me. And when your body began to change, you weren't mine anymore. The more you grew, the less you were here in this world for me."

"I used to be your doll."

"You looked great as a kid," she said. "Everyone said so."

"You dressed me up however you liked, straightened my hair, cut it short. My therapist says it wasn't healthy."

"Children are always for their parents. And they'll never be happy with any of it."

"I don't think you should have been a mother."

"I loved being your mother."

I shouldn't have said it. But then I couldn't stop myself.

"You never prioritized me, you didn't even pay much attention except in that you wanted me to be good and obedient."

"I prioritized you enough to move here. To leave everything behind."

I'd heard this all my life.

"That's not true."

"How would you know?"

"You came here for you, too."

"You think I wanted to leave my family and friends behind? To come here and work overnight at gas stations and sell mascara at the mall when I could have just stayed in Iran and been comfortable?"

"I don't think you were comfortable. After everything that happened, you couldn't stay either. Maybe you felt like you had to say it was for me because that made it selfless."

"Having a child is a selfless act."

"I disagree," I said. "It's selfish."

"You don't have children. And now you're too old to have them."

It didn't hurt my feelings because I didn't want children. But I saw what she was doing.

"I'm not too old," I said.

"You're single. It's too late for you."

"Having children is selfish."

"I prayed for you," she said.

"You prayed for me? What? To have a husband?"

"I prayed to have you. I wanted a daughter badly. And then before I had you, I dreamed of you. A little girl with big eyes and brown hair in pigtails and bangs. My grandfather called to me in my dream. You were holding his hand, and he handed you to me."

"You never told me that."

"You don't know everything I've gone through."

"If you could do it all over again, would you have me?"

"Absolutely," she said.

"That can't be true," I said. "I think you'd do it all differently. You'd be an actress. You'd live a glamorous life. When you had me it was kind of your only option."

"Maybe the language barrier makes it hard for us to communicate. You don't understand me."

Most of our arguments ended with her saying this. My Farsi was good but it wasn't nuanced, and she took advantage of that. When my father was executed and our family broke, my mother and I became lost to each other, bonded only by responsibility and dependence. The more I realized she was not mine, the less I became hers.

The 1970 film *Wanda*, written and directed by Barbara Loden (who also plays the lead), opens with Wanda making her way to a rural courthouse to give up custody of her children to her ex-husband. She doesn't have any money and she's not so put together, not as we'd expect a mother to be. She gets there late, with rollers in her hair and casual clothes. She doesn't fight to keep the children, doesn't embrace them or say hello or goodbye to them. They are tiny things left to the world. Their own mother, the person whose body created them, right there but untouchable.

    Wanda spends the entirety of the film living for herself. She's neither happy nor thriving. Mostly she just falls into situations, hoping she'll be cared for. All she wants is to be okay. She doesn't want to be a mother. If her ex-husband and his wife had offered to take her in, she likely would have gone with them.

    I never wanted to be a mother. Even as a girl, when my girlfriends talked about how many kids they wanted, I'd surprise them by saying none.

In the room we were sharing, I took out my camera and snapped a few pictures of my mother. She was caught off-guard, unsure of what was happening. She waved off the camera.

    "I have to take some pictures of you," I said.

    I hadn't told her I had an agenda for our trip. I was working on a series about home, wanted to explore my relationship to her through a lens. I had been inspired by the work of Mickalene Thomas, whose mother was her muse. They'd had a difficult relationship, which Thomas documented in a short film she'd made about her mother. It seemed that the portraits had brought them together again. The work had become their common language. What I saw in those paintings and photographs, what I'd watched in the documentary—maybe it was intimacy?—made me feel like I'd been turned upside down.

    I didn't say any of this to my mother. I wouldn't be able to convey that to her.

    "I don't look right," she said.

    "It's not about that," I said. "And, you're always beautiful."

    "Don't you need lights for a portrait?"

    "I'm doing this a little differently."

"Let me get ready, at least."

"Why don't I take a few of you in the robe, just as you are."

She didn't hate this. She'd always wanted to be a star.

I put her in different positions around the room. Then we took a few pictures of her putting on her makeup.

"So, this is a little weird, but I actually need to photograph your body," I said. "Without clothes."

I wasn't sure how she'd receive this.

"That's fine," she said.

She took off the robe.

"Everything?" she asked.

"If that's okay with you."

She pulled down her underwear. I put my camera very near her and examined the disembodied flesh, saw all the white hairs. Her belly, covered with stretch marks, was soft and uneven. Through the lens it looked like a map. The topography of my beginnings.

I captured as many pieces of her as I could, her hands, her knees. I tried to meet the tenderness of her offering with my own gentleness, which never came easy. I asked her to pose for me, however felt most comfortable. She sat on a chair with her legs crossed, her arms still on each armrest and looked straight into the lens.

Darla had asked if I'd be interested in going to Joshua Tree to pick up a lamp from the house of one of her clients. I didn't want to leave my mother, but she said she wouldn't mind a few hours on her own.

In the hotel courtyard, a bride and groom were taking their wedding photos, deliriously happy. We stopped to watch them.

"What is it about weddings?" Darla said.

I thought for a moment. I loved weddings and often cried when I attended them. We continued toward the lobby.

"It's the hope, I think," I finally said. "There are only a few instances in life when hope is so perfectly tangible. Weddings and—"

She cut me off, "—childbirth."

"Exactly," I said.

"Are you or have you been married?"

"Once. I'm divorced now. You?"

"Technically no. But also yes. I got married before gay marriage was legal. We did the whole thing, a ceremony, a big party, a honeymoon. Then when we got home; I had to keep filling out all of my paperwork as single."

"Did you wear a wedding dress?"

She laughed. "Can you imagine?"

"Did your wife?"

"She did. It was her thing."

We were in her car. The sun was still scalding and bright,"

"I got legally married—to a man. Which was a mistake. We eloped. I didn't wear a wedding dress."

"Why did you get married?" she said.

"I thought that was what I was supposed to do. I was young and I was scared of losing everyone."

We'd veered off the main road to a desolate dirt one, surrounded by cacti and Joshua trees. There was no one ahead of us and no one coming in the opposite direction. She drove fast, with confidence, as we continued to talk. Suddenly, out of nowhere, a coyote darted out from the bushes right in front of our car. She braked hard, and we lurched forward as the car stopped and swerved.

She grabbed my hand and held it tightly. We sat, with just the sound of our breathing.

By the time I looked up the coyote was gone, disappeared in the bushes on the other side of the street. Just then, a pack of coyotes appeared. Eight in total. All of them white with piercing eyes and an elegant gait. I wished I could go to them.

They walked slowly, very near the car, following behind the one we'd almost hit.

"They're beautiful," I said. "But this feels apocalyptic."

"In some indigenous cultures you're not supposed to cross the path of the coyote," she said. "It's bad luck. Or it means that someone is deceiving you."

I hoped no misfortune would befall us. But I liked this adventure, being here with Darla.

"The coyotes are a little like brides," I said.

"How so?"

"Their white fur. It's the wedding dress we can't look away from. Two people in suits or just ordinary dresses, it doesn't have the same power."

"Virginal. The opposite of hopeful."

"Do you know about Pippa Bacca?"

"I don't," she said.

"She was an Italian performance artist who wore a wedding gown and decided to walk across Eastern Europe through the Balkans to promote peace.

"All along the way, she walked and hitchhiked—there was another artist with her; the two of them went together, but I don't remember the other artist's name. Anyway, they hitchhiked, and then at every stop she had arranged through her network to meet midwives and she'd wash their feet with this bar of soap she had made with ash from a bonfire where she'd invited everyone she knew and asked them to burn something for her, for good luck for her journey."

"That's hopeful."

"But this isn't a hopeful story."

"No?"

"Somewhere outside of Istanbul she got into a car with a guy who took her into the woods, raped and killed her. He stole her video camera. The one she'd used to document the journey. He erased the work she was making and used the camera to record his nephew's wedding a few days later."

"It almost feels intentional. You know, how it ended and everything, like she had a role in it."

"Are you saying she deserved it?" I said.

"Well, no. But she was performing virginity and all of human history is about man's ownership of women's virginity."

We both laughed.

"I don't know why we're laughing," I said.

I stayed in the car as Darla went in to meet with her client and get the lamp. The sun was setting behind the mountains to the west, still fully round and low to the ground, an enormous and perfectly orange egg yolk. The mountains had become varying shades of brown and gray, their details obscured in the dark. Layered before and behind one another, they looked like hills in a shadowbox.

As the sun set the Joshua trees all around me looked more and more like people with their arms raised in shock or resignation. Finally the front door opened and Darla walked out holding a large box. The client, a woman in her sixties or seventies, was right behind her. She patted Darla on the back as they said goodbye, and Darla headed toward the car. I didn't see exactly what happened because I was looking at my phone, but I looked up when I heard Darla yelp and saw that she had fallen. I ran out of the car as she picked herself up. The client was tending to the box a few feet away.

"It's shattered," the client kept repeating. "It's shattered. It's destroyed."

I thought my mother and I would have dinner that night, but when I got back to the hotel room she had already eaten.

"Did you get room service?" I asked.

"I ate at the bar."

It had never occurred to me that my mother could sit alone at a hotel bar.

"Oh it was wonderful," she said, and lit up. "I had steak frites and a martini."

I don't think I'd ever seen my mother drink anything stronger than a single beer.

"Oh, and I saved that little girl's life."

"You what?!"

"Of course they'd brought her out to dinner," she said, still annoyed.

"Okay. So what happened?"

"She was drinking her milk from a bottle and she choked. The mother was screaming for help, the father was calling 911, and everyone else was frozen. I've never been in a room like that, it was totally silent. The girl was turning blue, so I ran up, grabbed her out of her mother's arms, turned her over, pulled down her pants and stuck my finger up her butt."

"That can't be true."

"Absolutely is."

"How did you know to do that?"

"You almost died once, choking on milk. And your father grabbed you and did that. He saved your life. It was terrifying, to think I might lose you."

She was already getting ready for bed, but I coaxed her to walk the grounds with me. It took some convincing, but she came. The night was temperate, and the cicadas competed with the wedding party. In a large cabana some distance away, we saw the bride and groom and guests dancing wildly. We found a fire pit with empty chairs around it. She stretched her hands toward the fire and I saw again the paper-thin skin I'd photographed earlier.

A waiter came to take our order.

"Martinis, I think," I said.

"I don't want a martini. Do they have Kahlúa?" she asked.

"Yes, we do," the waiter said.

"I'll have that with a decaf coffee," she said.

"Would you still like a martini?" the waiter asked me.

"It's not the same without her. How about a hot cocoa with a shot of rum."

"Would you like a s'mores box?" the waiter asked.

"What is that?" my mother said.

"A very American thing," I said. "It's so fun."

"Most American things aren't very fun."

I showed her how to roast her marshmallow. She wasn't patient enough to hold hers away from the fire. She preferred immersing it and eating the singed part.

"How was your date?" she asked.

We'd never talked about it. But of course she knew.

"It was nice," I said.

"Tell me what you like about her," she said.

ORAL HISTORY / PETER TRACHTENBERG

THE CHIMNEY GIRL

In Westbeth she's known mostly as the Chimney Girl, so that's what I'll call her. She was a child of the building, as was the tenant who first told me her story. Her parents were musicians. By the time she was twelve she was already showing signs of trouble, though those signs may not have been apparent—may not even have existed—until later. The past looks different when viewed in the glare of the future, which magnifies irregularities and small disfigurements while at the same time blinding you to everything else. Afterward you remember only the disfigurements, the issues. At the time, however, she was just a girl. In pictures she's quite pretty.

It was summer; a cousin came to visit. The cousin was older, already a young woman, but making up for the difference in their ages was the fact that the Chimney Girl was a New Yorker, which adds five years to any child's age, and lived in a labyrinthine fortress of artists, some cool, some just weird. Still, she wanted to impress her cousin, and so one night she took her up thirteen stories to the roof. She showed her the city the way another child would show a visitor her room: the grid of glowing streets that to the south became a web of diagonal and zigzag strands; the ghostly high-rises thrusting toward the moon; the softly lapping river where late ferries glided between the banks. Perhaps feeling that wasn't enough, she pointed to the chimney that rose another two dozen feet overhead. There was a ladder attached to it. The tenant who told me this story remembered that the kids she'd grown up with used to mess around on it. The young girl climbed the ladder. I don't know if the cousin climbed behind her or watched from below. At the top, the girl struck a pose, maybe heroic, maybe clownish. Then she pitched backward and disappeared soundlessly into the chimney's gaping mouth.

The cousin froze.

An instant later she was brought back into her body. Maybe she took the elevator, maybe she leapt down the stairs three at a time. She pounded on the door to the apartment and told the girl's father what had happened. He called 911. Some firemen arrived; Westbeth's super led them down into the basement and then to a steel door that opened into the base of one of several chimneys. A lieutenant poked his fingers through a crack, and a small hand appeared on the other side. He jumped back. He hadn't expected to find someone alive: people were killed by falling three stories, and this girl had fallen more than thirteen. When the door was broken open, he saw eyes and a mouth floating in the sooty darkness. It might've been an image from a cartoon. You hear of people laughing in relief, even people who are used to opening doors and finding the dead behind them—maybe especially such people.

The blackened face spoke. "Am I dead?"

She had fallen 180 feet and landed in a mound of soot and ash, years, maybe decades of it, soot so deep she'd had to claw her way up to the surface. The soot had saved her. The lieutenant thought she'd fallen headfirst and landed on her back. At the hospital she was found to have a dislocated hip and multiple fractures. In the storyteller's memory, the injuries were worse than that; she thought the girl had also suffered lung damage from inhaling ash. "I think she ended up having a pretty serious drug problem.

Whether that was a factor before or after I don't know. She must've been on lots of painkillers. Her parents live in Westbeth. I don't know where she lives. I don't know what her deal is. After that the building got wise to some of these things. They clipped the ladders, they put up fences so that kids couldn't crawl into places. There've been many generations of kids who've grown up in Westbeth."

The story has become part of the folklore of the building, a cautionary tale for parents, a legend passed down to the next generation of Westbeth children, who hearing it may feel not just frightened but also secretly thrilled. Because, after all, the Chimney Girl lived.

Grace Bergere's musician parents moved into Westbeth when she was eight. They divorced when she was eleven. After that, she shuttled back and forth between her mother's apartment on the first floor and her father's on the sixth.

Bergere is vague about dates. "I attribute my brain to a few things, one of which is the accident. I hit the ground at seventy-something miles per hour."

As a young child, she used to visit a boy on the eighth floor who'd rigged an intricate network of plastic tubes in his room: you'd drop a marble in one end and hear it rattle through the system until it popped out someplace else. Sometimes they'd go out into one of the narrow hallways and brace their feet against one wall and their hands against the opposite one and inch their way up almost to the ceiling, then drop down onto a mattress they'd dragged there for that purpose.

Elsewhere she was unhappy, especially after she transferred to a new school: "I never did well in school, I was always a weird outcast. And I didn't have many friends. And then when I got to IS 89 because PS 3 was a hippy school where we were fingerpainting and singing all day long, and now we're at a math school . . . where I didn't learn any math. I felt stupid and chubby and stinky. And I had acne, and nobody wanted to talk to me."

She was twelve. Her cousin Lily visited from California. "It felt nice to have someone sort of my age to hang out with. I mean, she wasn't really my age, but she feels like my peer, and I didn't have any siblings. I don't remember what led to us being on the roof except that I thought it would be interesting for Lily. And it was nighttime. It was dark.

"I did not have a cell phone, I did not have video games. The way that I knew how to play was using my body and climbing things. I'd been climbing things my whole life, you know. Like in Central Park we would climb the rocks, and trees, and buildings, and whatever. I've talked to a lot of people from New York, and that's how they are. So anyway, I saw the ladder. And I didn't know it was a chimney, either. I don't think I would have done what I did if I'd known there was a hole at the top of it. And, by the way, I didn't slip and fall. I was just mistaken about the nature of what I was doing. I hate to sound like an asshole, but I mean, I'm a juggler. Climbing a ladder and sitting on something is not challenging to me. And it wasn't challenging to me when I was twelve."

It's here that Bergere's story departs from the official version you can read in *The New York Times*, though you can see how it might drive a fact-checker crazy. It still sounds more truthful. No one was with her when she fell, and if she can't entirely say what happened she can come closer to it than anybody else. "Okay, what happened was I climbed the ladder, and I put my hand out to sit on it. I thought it was asphalt, the blackness. And I put my whole weight onto nothing. It didn't occur to me that there wouldn't be anything there. It never occurred to me, you know, that there would be an industrial-size chimney in New York City in my building, which is an apartment building, because I'm twelve. In my mind, I thought it was a tower. I don't know why there would be a tower, but I thought it was a tower."

The hole was as wide as her outstretched arms. "I remember I put my hands out. I was falling, but I didn't *know* that I was falling because it was so . . . I didn't know what the fuck was going on. See, if I had known it was a chimney and I'd slipped and fell, I think I'd be dead. Because I was . . . I was so relaxed. It felt like I was falling through water. It felt like water because the pressure of the air hitting me felt like . . . like a . . . *substance*. I just remember it felt like I was touching something and something was cradling me. It was just the air pressure. And then I remember hitting the ground. And they calculate that I fell for a few seconds. You know, I mean, it's pretty high."

It was 180 feet.

"And I think what happened was I made a full rotation. I don't remember what part of my body hit first, but I think I went in headfirst, and then my hips kind of balanced me out. My feet and then my ass, and then my shoulders and then my head. If I was tense or flailing, I could have landed on my head. I remember when I hit the ground, I heard my neck break. Everything was white. And it was like, in my head there was just this crazy, loud, static sound. It felt pretty psychedelic—just the whiteness and the crazy fucking sound, and my whole body was kind of vibrating.

"And I wasn't scared because I didn't know what the hell was going on. I knew something really bad had happened, but I didn't know what it was. And I wasn't scared because it had already happened. There was a part of me that was like, *steadfastly calm* about it. Like I knew that whatever was happening was normal. I know that sounds like a lot of crazy, weird lies, but it really felt wholly okay with me because I wasn't in pain. Like my brain had shut off my pain sensors . . . like I'd lost all sense of my body. It didn't feel like I was in a body at all. I was like, 'Damn, what the fuck is happening to me? This isn't so bad, I guess.'

"It was completely black. And what I was saying before, which is kind of important, is that . . . and I know this sounds too much like a movie . . . but I really did think of my mother. That really was the main thing driving me, the desire to not pass out and die. If I had done nothing, I would have died because

I had ashes shoved down into my mouth and chest, and I couldn't breathe at all. And it turns out that one-and-a-half lungs had collapsed. So I had half of one lung working. And I remember I had to remove all the soot out of my throat. I couldn't cough or anything, so I was using my hand to pull the shit out of my throat. And at this point my skin was burning. My whole skin was on fire, I think because of shock. But I didn't feel any pain in my back yet; it turns out I broke my back in, I think, eight places. And my hip, I dislocated my hip. And my shoulder, too. And I had all kinds of fractures all over the place. And I ruptured my spleen. I don't know what that does.

"So then I sat up, and that helped with breathing, and I leaned against the wall, because it was like a big chamber and then a little echo chamber, from what I remember. And there was a hole, and I could see the basement light through the hole. The wall had been cemented shut. If no one had been with me [on the roof], I would be dead. No one would have known where I was. So, I started putting my mouth up to the hole because the air down there was so fucking disgusting. I used my arm and I broke the hole bigger with my arm. And I put my hand out, and I was waving my hand around and trying to breathe.

"I think while I was still kind of on my back, my cousin went down to get my dad. She didn't really know what happened because she just saw that I was climbing that thing, and then she turned away, and then I wasn't there anymore. She didn't know it was a chimney either. And as soon as she told my dad what happened, he knew what it meant. And he was really freaking out, obviously. And he got up on the ladder and waved his phone down at me. Because, you know, he thought I was dead. Everyone thought I was dead. He was the first person to know I wasn't dead. He's like, 'Are you alive? Are you okay?' I was like, 'I'm okay. I broke my leg or something.' The only thing I knew is that I couldn't move my leg.

"He told me he called the fire department, so I wasn't really that scared. I knew that I was okay. But apparently the firemen didn't believe him at all . . . that I was okay. They thought he was hallucinating or something. And I remember when the firemen came, they told me to back up from the entrance, and they broke the door with a sledgehammer. The EMTs dragged me out, and I just wanted water immediately. And they won't let you have water because if they have to do surgery, they don't want you to vomit. They laid me out on the stretcher. Man, I don't know how this happened, I think they were probably nervous. They didn't know what to expect. But they started forcing my leg down, and my leg was broken. It was dislocated, it wasn't in the socket, and they were pushing it down. I remember telling them, 'I can't put my leg down!' They were like, '*You have to!*' and I was like, '*I can't!*' A piece of my hip was broken.

"I remember they took me up, and I remember looking up at the ceiling in the lobby and looking around, and everyone was standing around and looking at me. Like people in the building. And then I was in the ambulance, and I remember the ambulance guy had to cut my clothes off me. And I didn't want him to cut my clothes off me because I liked my pants. And he's talking to me about Barney, Barney the dinosaur. And I was like, 'How old do you think I am?' I was immediately giving them shit. They took me to the hospital, and they had to put me through an MRI, and I had three or four piercings in my ear cartilage, and they had to take them out. I remember yelling at them about that.

"They took me to Bellevue, and then NYU. Up until this point, I was not in any pain. And then I remember, I must have finally passed out. I think they must have given me something. And then I remember I woke up and I was all alone in this room. And all of a sudden, I was in fucking agony. My whole body was just screaming. I was screaming. And I didn't know why I was alone, either. I was just alone in this room. I think my parents were at the door, but I couldn't see them. And I was just screaming.

"And then I was in the ICU for a while, at least a month. They never did any surgery on me, they just relocated my hip and put it in traction where they put the bar through your knee. It was like being held up in the air. And then they had me in a brace in bed, so it was just time. And they had me do these exercises, where I would blow into a tube."

This was probably an incentive spirometer, meant to help her reflate and strengthen her lungs.

"And they had me on morphine. And that's a whole other story. I remember, I *loved* the hospital. To this day I love the hospital. I love going to the hospital. I feel like I'm being taken care of when I go to the hospital. I have really positive body associations with the hospital and the doctors because they just had me on morphine. I would go to sleep with that [pump] just rigid in my grip. And I needed it, I really needed it. I was so fucked. The first time I went through withdrawal was in the hospital. They said that I was having a psychotic episode, because they transferred me [to a rehab facility] and they didn't tell them that I was on morphine. So not only was my back shattered, and I was still in a brace, I had to wear a brace for a year after that. But I was in excruciating pain. And I was going through withdrawal. And I was twelve."

Grace Bergere is thirty now. She's a working musician whose first album was released by Casa Gogol Records in 2024. Her songs are suspended between the grim wisdom of their lyrics and the shimmering lushness of their harmonies and lent authority by the directness of her voice, which is devoid of melismata or any of the other techniques singers use to court the sympathy and admiration of their audience. It just states its case. As one of her songs puts it: "I did nothing wrong."

FICTION / TRANSLATED FROM THE CATALAN BY LAWRENCE VENUTI

ACCIDENTS
ANNA BALLBONA

For Grandma, things would occasionally get dark. We'd be eating dinner at home—in that feeble light from the austerity you didn't choose—and suddenly we'd hear a boom. We'd all jump up. Unlike the dining room, the kitchen was lit by a blinding fluorescent fixture that always flickered two or three times before it started working. On the terrazzo floor, between a metal chair and the secondhand table, lay Grandma, stretched out, unconscious. Tawdry furniture always makes a bigger racket than the normal kind. When she fell, her black skirt, the one that hits mid-calf, had ridden up above her knee, exposing her slip and thighs and dull brown stockings. It was pretty disgusting. Sometimes she would pee on herself.

She had completely lost consciousness. "Things got dark": This expression, which I heard only in my house, used to fill me with horror. And I would ask myself whether things could get dark for someone else as well, for my brother, say, or for me.

I find it hard to pin down the next moves—who revived her, who dampened her face with cool water, who addressed some words to her and sat her up. The fact is, my mother usually had to do everything since she was the only one who could function in this kind of situation.

"She had another fall."

"So what happened to her?"

"Things got dark."

The formula was repeated over and over again whenever they tried to explain the incident.

When Grandma broke her femur and needed a zimmer to get around, she'd cut a path through the house every day, multiple times, back and forth, with a discipline worthy of admiration. Her circulation was bad, and her health, not just her balance, was very precarious. You had to help her stand up and sit down, and sometimes she would sink back into the chair. To get down a flight of stairs she needed two people, one on each side, or they would carry her in a chair, cradled in their arms. One of her legs was longer than the other, something that made her wear an orthopedic boot with a lift (it looked like a football player's shoe to me). More food for this world of freakish, fantastical creatures. I didn't know any other kid whose grandmother was such a basket case. And our other grandparents, my mother's parents, who could have formed a contrast—they'd died before I was born.

Sometimes my mother would wake me in the morning to walk behind Grandma just in case she lost her balance. I wasn't overjoyed; I didn't even have time to eat breakfast. From the moment she appeared at the end of the corridor we had to watch she didn't run into furniture or block our way. We—she and I—had to mark out a completely unobstructed path. One stifling hot day, when the emptiness in my stomach turned more obtrusive than ever, I became aware that my head was spinning until all of a sudden things got really dark and I dropped to the floor. Grandma had to park herself by the wall as best she could, like someone who pulls up to unload the car.

"Come quick! Mila fell!"

My mother arrived. She immediately propped up my legs and gave me a little water. Since then the darkness has rarely come over me. When I feel the slightest dizziness, I immediately drop to the floor to prevent the state I must avoid no matter what. I'm totally spooked by that time I lost consciousness.

For Grandma, however, things got dark so many times. And the ruckus over what you least expected—the plunge to the floor, the way it shuffled around the metal chair and formica table and sent all of us running—I'll never get it out of my head. Nor the times she woke up in the middle of the night, gripped by a coughing fit, breathless from a worsening case of chronic bronchitis, and my mother, her daughter-in-law, would get up to care for her, always the first one, as if she had a sensor, or the finest sense of hearing, or a sixth sense attuned to the woman's vital signs. Later my brother and I would get up and we'd see her lips, a discordant purple, on a face red with coughing, her eyes transfigured into orbs. We knew it would all end with another night in the hospital.

We are the trials and tribulations we share, the world we alone know and very often we alone can understand. There is loneliness in knowing this certainty, which at least offers us refuge. Perhaps this is why I feel the need to put all these scenes in order. It's as if in stacking up these lines, one on top of the other, I align my universe a little, the oddities and innovations that have driven me and brought me this far. It's as if you domesticate the world you come from, that past I kept in a room somewhere, so that one day I might present it to my daughter beautifully decorated. Look, I'll tell her: Here's grandpa's artificial leg, here's my father's curses, here's Grandma's orthopedic shoe, here are the contradictions, it was the Wild West and I shot from the hip... But why tell her? Won't the darkness travel across generations on its own?

Not long ago I dreamed I was walking behind Grandma again and watching she didn't lose her balance. We were in a cul-de-sac, extremely tense. I was trying to make her stand up straight and not fall. She got up from the sofa, then she went to the bathroom, then she parked at the wall. Tottering Grandma played the leading role, poor woman, in a torment that lasted till I woke up—although she didn't fall.

This nightmare resonates with the turmoil from the night I spent with Jonás in Tenerife. "It was only a one-night stand; these things happen at business conventions. We haven't talked in weeks. I shouldn't make a big thing out of it."

I repeat this mantra to myself. It would've been just another brief encounter, so easy, if not for what transpired after I got back: The new development certified by the aseptic notary (otherwise known as the gynecologist), the joy shared with my partner Simó, the streak of unleashed truculence, the inner confusion, the question of whether I should do something or just keep quiet. Do I explain it to Simó or forget about it since I'm pregnant? Memories I can't fathom, bizarre dreams, cars run off the road, tragedies by the bucketload. And Grandma staring at me, filling me with guilt. I was bursting into tears, I felt nauseous, I didn't want to see anyone, I'd wake up late, I didn't respond to messages from friends. . .

 I didn't hit bottom till the third month, when I had to make a decision. Mila, you're pregnant: Is this what you want? What would be the point of explaining it to anyone? Besides, who says you have to explain everything or know it all? What we don't know can't turn into a problem unless we want it to be a problem. And maybe the gift—or mystery—of survival lies in turning a deaf ear to the racket you're told to put up with because for centuries we've gotten used to living with it and to refuse is unacceptable. Guilt is what they call the roar. You can only surf that roiling sea in your Sunday best. I was left with the compulsion to scrutinize myself, especially on days when I had some free time—a solemn affectation destined to torture me with the thought that I'd inherited some negative residue, derived from my parents' factory jobs and activated whenever I let my guard down. But on other days I can't stop seeing the comedy of certain details suspended in the atmosphere of my childhood.

 Today has to be that kind of day. One of Grandma's classic phrases crosses my mind: "We're born into this world to suffer."

 Grandma routinely made this declaration. She had obviously suffered a great deal, but the thing is, she'd say it as often as she could, with no fear of wasting it. Some shadows are so dark that, depending on their particular slant, they can be transformed into black humor. When Grandma started to catch cold and had to stay in bed because she was doing a lot of huffing and puffing, the phrase would return: "We're born into this world to suffer."

 Deep down, if I went to bed with Jonás, it was because of an intimate, even unconscious impulse to rebel against this imposed lament (among other things, no doubt).

 When we'd try to comfort Grandma because she had to take a course of antibiotics which, along with her seven other pills (anti-inflammatory drugs, vitamins, stomach-coating medication), had suppressed her appetite, she would sigh histrionically, as if no one could understand her, as if she were ready for the final act. And she would grumble with resignation: "That's very easy for you to say. You don't know what I suffer."

I don't know when these phrases were embedded in her speech or whether she would say them before the accident. I hadn't yet entered the world when that happened. At this point, though, whatever she says doesn't surprise me.

On a Saturday afternoon in June, when Grandma would usually go shopping in town, she walked under the highway by the side of the road. From the neighborhood this route could be covered in fifteen to twenty minutes on foot. She had done it hundreds of Saturdays.

Grandma knew the way to town by heart. I myself learned it decades later when I'd return home from school or go out on weekend nights. For us, "under the bridge" was a concrete geographic point with its own features, which could be sketched in detail. When someone joked that if you met a nasty-looking guy under a bridge you'd run away, our bridge would unequivocally come to mind. It wasn't a question of some mythical object. The underside of a highway is considered a terrifying place. Sheltered from the traffic that flows furiously overhead, you hear only a murmur that gets louder when a number of trucks are linked together. At night, the broad columns festooned with coarse, wordy graffiti cast foreboding shadows, and you feel they hide phantoms ready to pounce on you.

That Saturday afternoon the driver of a van, who they reckon was distracted by the construction work on the bridge, hit my grandmother. Then he fled. An indeterminate length of time had passed before a neighbor found her sprawled out, unconscious, half dead. He loaded her into his car as best he could and took her to the district hospital in Barcelona. With a cell phone the incident would inevitably have been different. The neighbor left her at the hospital without knowing the woman he had aided was an acquaintance, someone who would buy from his butcher shop. He learned about it later. She was covered in blood and blackened by the impact of the hit-and-run. The man who rescued her thought she was a gypsy.

At the hospital they induced a coma so she could endure the pain from her injuries. We had to wait and see how her body reacted, pushed to a brutal threshold. In my house we never referred to it as anything but "the accident." It marked a before and after, adding a stretch of time that Grandma would live as a gift. She had several broken ribs. A body full of purple bruises was the first thing her husband and sons saw when they entered the ICU. She was unrecognizable. She hadn't yet reached fifty. After a couple of months, she awoke and started a slow recuperation.

"The doctor put it like this"—I often heard her explain to my mother—"Saint Peter didn't want me, so he closed the gates of heaven."

Years later, when the repeated attacks of bronchitis sent her periodically to the hospital, requiring more and more X-rays, the nurses were appalled to see her rib cage. It must have looked like a cluster of stars supported by some miraculous engineering.

"Every time they saw those ribs, they would throw up their hands, and we'd have to tell them it was from the accident she'd suffered."

Grandma survived with several excruciating after-effects. I recognized it from a scar that crossed her left eye and eyebrow. My parents said it was nothing compared to the disfigurement she displayed in the early years. They were devastated because she also lost her sight in that eye. The bowel surgery affected other parts of her body: Apart from the rib cage, she couldn't lift her right arm above the shoulder, and in the upper part of her back you could make out a number of hollows, as if they had been squeezed.

"You're working, then suddenly they tell you something like this happened." My father could barely stammer out the memory. Inside his peculiar maze for finding words, amid the fitful phrases and skimpy resources, you intuited the shock from weeks of terrifying uncertainty.

Years later I would attempt to put the pieces in place like someone who views a clumsily deformed face in a cubist painting.

"Let's see, Grandma. Raise your arm." I would tease her, although without derision, doing it only because I was curious whether everybody but her could raise their right arm.

Grandma complied—it was just another way of being for her—and she lifted her arm up to her shoulder, not a millimeter higher. The amazing thing is how precise the result of an accident can be. Or an earthquake. Just thinking about it gives you a jolt. The quake leaves cracks no matter how much cement you pour.

They say her head had to be sewn up again, and ever since she has suffered from bad circulation: Swollen legs, veins protruding from her skin, purple bruises that appear right after she gets a bump, and a bloodstream that doesn't reach every part of her brain or every joint. I now realize that next to that misfortune, which was like a ghostly presence, saying things would get dark seems like a lame joke. Which might be the best way to take it.

Kate Shepherd, *Selfie*

Kate Shepherd, *Helena Lights*

FICTION

ASTRAEA
KATE KRUIMINK

I. It was six o'clock in the morning and the ocean was pooled dark glass. The sky was nothing, but also nothing else, not cloud nor sun nor moon. There was a slow creak in the air.

    The maybe-friend Sarah Ward had poisoned herself again in the night and was convulsing in the hospital below. The other women in the pen had made flocks of themselves, bonnets fluttering, all done up to their necks in their coarse grays and browns like common pigeons. Even that terrible old madwoman had found company. But without Sarah Ward, the girl sat alone.

"I give you a riddle! What is neither here nor there?" called the madwoman to the eye-rolling friends about her. "What is trees where no trees grow? What is thirst in water?"

"No one wants riddles," called back a tolerant young mother from a saner circle.

The three women drystoning the deck raced one another into the final corner, laughing, and stood to stretch their arms back and forth.

Somehow all the women had got the measure of each other already—had done it almost immediately, just by clapping eyes on one another—but the girl did not know anything about any of them, really, aside from a few observances that, when put together, did not make a pattern she might begin to anticipate. She certainly did not know what to make of the maybe-friend Sarah Ward, who sat with her except on inscrutable occasions when she would sit away from her and not look at her and talk very animatedly to some Northerner or Welshwoman or other instead, and who whispered filthy things hot into her ear that she thought the girl would need to know, and who lay very restless beside her at night, annoying the other two women who shared their berth, and who gave the girl food from her own plate because she thought she, the girl, had become too thin and colourless, and who kept hurting herself, rending her flesh and bringing her secret insides right out into the brisk sea air with such purpose she was like a hysterical monk offering utter bodily abjection up to God. But Sarah did not much care for God because he did not much care for her, because if he did she would be in her natural state, she said, which was of course a palace with fine eiderdown quilts.

That doctor, that Scotsman, did not approve of any of them and especially he did not approve of Sarah. His disapproval had not yet cured her, but still he was trying it.

Someone began to sing "The Bitter Withy." The chaplain did not often allow singing abovedecks, lest it draw the sailors' attention, and when he did it was only hymns. He was forever creeping about, but now he stopped his creeping and straightened. The singing woman was not Margaret Muir with the voice of cream and honey, but still it was pleasant to hear her. *Our Saviour asked his mother dear / If he might play at ball*, she sang, but the chaplain gave a cry and strode to her, incredulous.

"Jesus Christ did not play at ball," he told her, voice trembling, neck all red.

The singer stopped, biting her next word in half. "But it is religious," the girl heard her whisper, as he stalked away.

The chaplain was very bad at religion. Worse than the women. The afternoon before, he had come down and read to them while their dinner got cold. He had done the reading that begins *Judge not, lest ye be judged*. It had a nice ring to it, but the effect of it was that all hundred or so women and girls closed their ears to him, because obviously they had already been judged, and therefore it followed they now might judge freely. That was so evident they did not even need to discuss it afterward. They simply exchanged intellectual glances over cold mutton.

A girl rose from a circle of other girls and staggered to the railing. She crouched down and sat there with her arms wrapped around her middle. "Mary, what are you about now?" called one of the others. She did not reply, but instead knelt and bent forward until her head was touching the deck. She started rifling through her skirt, hiking it up, scrabbling underneath, crying. The others giggled uneasily.

"Come now," said a woman with a stern voice, rising and going to her. "Stop that." But the girl only cried louder.

"It's out of me!" she said. "It's hanging out of me!"

"What, girl?"

"I think it is my womb!" she cried, and sat heavily. "Look!" She spread her knees and began to pull her skirts up. The woman slapped them down.

"There are men about!" she hissed, and indeed the sailors beyond the railings of their pen had raised their chins.

"And we don't want to see that, anyway," called someone else. The girl moaned and pulled herself upright and staggered off toward the hatch.

"I am going to see the doctor …" she said. The woman who had gone to her stood for a moment, hands on hips, shaking her head at their general company.

"She was too long in a dark cell, and has gone a little mad," she said. "She will not stop talking about her womb being pulled out of her." But where the girl had walked, there was a trail of poppy-red blood.

The terrible old madwoman heaved herself up. "I will go with her," she said, conversationally. "Wombs are like elbows to me. Very ordinary." She hobbled toward the hatch, but the chaplain, who had never shown so much personality in one morning, grabbed her arm tightly. His face was white and ungiving.

"Clean it, and then sit down in silence," he said. "I will not have this filth."

It was cold, but not as cold as it had been. The sky was too much of nothing to hold birds, and there were none in the lacework of rope above them. "We are beyond birds now," said the old madwoman, who could read the girl's mind through her face.

What is trees where no trees grow? What is thirst in water? the girl thought. There had been another part to it, but she could not remember it. There was no point when the answer was so obvious.

The glassy ocean had no underneath to it, not to the eye. It looked solid as a floor, like yet another surface that would require their cleaning. It gave the girl a sense of a great and dreary obligation, as if she must drop off the side of the ship and set out across this surface and keep slipping around on it, catching her ankles on the ridges and seams, trying to drystone it until she fell down and shriveled into a husk for lack of water. There was a poem about that, she thought, precisely that, but her mother had been a governess, and was therefore joyless and grey and with no heart for poetry, so the girl didn't know it beyond a few words and a suspicion that it might speak to her. Water, water, everywhere, were the words she knew, and that it was about being thirsty and unlucky. She did not want to be thinking of her mother. She needed to scrape her mind clean like a farrier scraping a horse's hoof, great pieces of filth and dead matter dropping away. It was not her mother's fault. She had done quite well with the girl. It was just that her mother was now a memory and the girl had decided that memory was not her business, unlike Sarah Ward, who would do nothing but dwell, which clearly did not do her any good. Water, water, the girl said to herself. Water, water, everywhere.

The children were quiet that morning. Their soft little heads were tucked into the bosoms and shoulders and laps of their mothers, letting the talk of the women dapple them like sun through leaves, there in that treeless place. The girl had a pang of wanting. It had occurred to her only quite recently that she did not belong amongst those soft little heads, that instead she was the bosom or the shoulder or lap, or ought to be.

Outside their pen the sun caught the bright buttons of the officers. Two of these men stood talking, squinting out to sea. Sailors made their repetitive movements, the hoistings, packings, scrubbings, passings, the hands-over-hands. She accidentally caught the eye of one of the ones who was always leering, and she looked away quickly.

There were other women near her there in their pen, but not with her. She had put herself by the bedding, which they brought up each morning to air. It was stinking, and an unpopular place to sit. The woman from Cork who did not like her was also near her and had set her shoulders in such a way as to communicate this dislike. She hated Sarah Ward too, which was a great comfort to the girl. Sarah Ward got terrible headaches because of something the woman had done to her.

The woman from Cork did not like the girl because she, the girl, had the Irish name of Maginn, but was in fact English not Irish, and yes her father was Irish but she didn't even really know the name of the place where he had come from. He was a physician too, like the Scottish doctor who was there with them to make sure none of them was ill in the incorrect way. The Scottish doctor's cures seemed quite harmful, and they certainly hurt, but it was the correct kind of hurting. Sarah Ward did the wrong kind.

Water, water, she thought. Water, water. Water, water, everywhere. Water and no more. Scape the mind clean. If you are looking for freedom, this oblivion is the freedom that is available to you. And you probably ought to take what you can get.

The young sailor, not the one who leered all the time, but the tall one with the easy way about him and the large hands and dark hair, came and found reason to pass into their pen and lean almost over her, tugging at something or other past her head. "Ah, get away!" said a woman, and the chaplain paced over to watch the sailor go back to his business. The young sailor had found occasion at other times to be near her too, and sometimes had whispered a thing or two, simple things made illicit, like that he was from Cornwall and his name was Peter Rowe, and that he would like to know where she was from and what her name was also.

A cry came muted from below, soaking upward through decks and beams to prickle the back of the girl's neck, but the only other person who gave any sign of having noticed it was the terrible old madwoman, for she turned her head in that moment.

———

Sarah Ward was seventeen. She said that they both ought to say they were twenty-one. The girl did not think she could pass for twenty-one. It was really very old. She was fifteen in body, but truly, as a person, she was far younger even than that. She was quite new.

II. A name is a kind of magic so strong that one or two hundred years ago you might have been hanged as a witch if you misused it, and one or two thousand years ago you wouldn't have been hanged but turned into a tree or something. Girls were forever being turned into trees back then. The name designates the thing, and without the name, the thing is impossible to hold in the mind. It shifts and disperses its particles into the air. And if you give the thing a new name, then it dies and is reconceived right in the instant of renaming, snuffed out and then poured into the world again with a new idea attached to what it might be. In any case, that is what had happened to the girl. She was not a tree, but she had been transformed, had been killed, in fact, killed by a tired clerk and reborn right back into the same body in one instant. There was a mistake with her name when it was being written down, and the mistake was that the clerk did not believe her when she said it, because it was too fanciful, too French. So he wrote down Maryanne instead, because that was more fitting, he said.

And so that was that: he killed the girl she had been, and then when he finished writing her into being, there she was before him where he sat with his lips all pursed, this fresh new creature without a sully or a mark who was called Maryanne Maginn. And was she not glad to have been given, now, at the ripe age of fifteen, an ordinary name that belonged to other women and girls too, probably hundreds upon hundreds of them, a crowd into which she could scurry and hide? And if memories from before she was killed and reborn imposed themselves upon her, she was perfectly entitled to say to herself, Well, that dark thing occurred to someone else, someone with a different name who is now dead, a name disapproved of, a name shamed, and not I. I am Maryanne Maginn, and the memories I have I may make anew. And if her body remembered the dark things that had happened to the dead girl with the French name by, for example, leaking milk from its breasts and settling a peculiar aching into its own arms—well, that had nothing to do with her.

"Wake up!" snapped the woman from Cork who did not like her. The girl who had been named Maryanne was already awake, but still she had nearly missed the call down to breakfast. There would be a pint of cocoa and endless dry biscuit, endless as the sea itself. She would maybe try to take some to Sarah Ward in the hospital if she got the courage up.

She crept down amongst the others in the way they had all learnt to walk, a little like riding a horse, bracing and swaying with the up and down and side to side of it. They went down the ladder one by one, then through the grated door into the long, low room. It always felt cluttered below, though they kept it clean and tidy. It was busy with their tables and benches down the middle, separated one from the next by rough pillars thick as trees, and their berths stacked two high all along both bulkheads, and the door to the hospital at the far end, from which came groans day and night. There was light in the daytime, for the hatches above were left open, but when the sun set it was black as the grave. They were not allowed a flame.

Each table sat eight women, and she found a corner by a pillar with some women who did not mind her. Here she might mouse away her portion of cocoa and biscuit brought by the women whose turn it was to do the food, she thought. But then that terrible old madwoman who babbled and giggled and pulled at her hair quite deliberately sat beside her, her yellow stench clouding over them both. "You are called Maryanne, are you not?" asked the old woman. They had been cleaning monitors together the previous week, the two of them and a few others, responsible until Sunday for cleaning up the night vomit because they were never ill themselves. There was less night vomit now, for everyone but one woman had grown accustomed to the drop and pull of the ship. The woman who was still ill might die, they were saying, for she could barely keep water down, and she had been moved from rolling about in her berth with her vomit slopping over her and her berthmates to trembling in one of the real beds bolted down in the sick bay with a pail beside her that she did not how to aim for.

The old woman knew already that the girl's name was Maryanne. Anyway, it was hardly worth asking, even if she had forgotten. It was provoking.

"Yes, I am," said the girl.

"Your bodice is wet," said the old woman, and Maryanne pressed her hands against her chest and yes, it was flowered with two warm and milky stains blooming into the crust of old ones again. "Wet wet wet," said the old woman.

"Perhaps one of the mothers will die and you may have her baby, for you have misplaced your own. I know. I know the imps took it away!" she said, wagging her finger. Maryanne sat there with her hands flat against herself and looked wildly around, not at the women, but anywhere else—the bulkheads, the table, the big pint cups going up and down in the women's fists, the flat pieces of sky and ocean outside the squares of light above.

"Oh, leave her be, Mary Christie," said an Irishwoman. This woman had an air tired but brave, with great green eyes and black-and-grey hair soft at her temples. She untied herself at her back and unwrapped her shoulders and passed a brown shawl over the old Englishwoman to Maryanne. "Wrap that about yourself, little girl, and do not mind Mrs. Christie," she said, and Maryanne did, and everything was salty and wrong, but then she reminded herself that it was nothing to do with Maryanne Maginn if her body leaked strange things at inopportune times, and that she could not possibly know what that meant because it belonged to someone who had been killed by a magical clerk. She returned to her breakfast and swallowed and swallowed and swallowed. And when the kind Irishwoman said, "It will pass soon, dear. It will all dry up, don't you worry," it did not even have anything to do with her at all, and so she smiled politely and remarked on the weather, which was in fact completely unremarkable and therefore as perfect as anything might possibly be outside Heaven to talk about. The shawl around her shoulders still smelt of the sheep which grew the wool.

"It sends some mad, you know," said the Irishwoman, after a pause.

"The weather?" asked Maryanne.

"No, girl," she said. "Not the weather."

"*I* am mad, Mrs. Beattie," said the terrible old woman, baring her teeth, or what remained of them. "*I* have been sent mad by the devil, for I am a witch."

"No, you are not," said the Irishwoman Beattie.

"Perhaps I am and perhaps I am not," said Mary Christie. "In the old days they would hang you or set fire to you for being a witch. Put screws on your fingers and pokers up you and rack you and then kill you badly even if you said you were not one, even if you denied it. But now that we are all enlightened, what they punish you for is saying you *are* a witch when really you are not one. So either I really am one, or I am a criminal," she said, and the women smiled despite themselves, there in their prison.

"You are putting it on so we will all think you interesting and so that the doctor will give you laudanum and tuck you up in one of those nice beds he has. But he is not watching now and we are all tired of your antics, and this young girl has done nothing to you, so please you be quiet," said the Irishwoman Beattie, but she was smiling too.

"Oh, well," said Mrs. Christie.

"We must all pass the time somehow," said the Irishwoman. The light brightened her bonnet. "And I am not Mrs. Beattie, for I never married."

Mrs. Christie snorted. "I cannot call you Miss. It is too terrible to be a miss with grey in your hair."

"I do not ask you to! My name is Joan. And you do well know this."

Mrs. Christie shook her head and turned her attention back to Maryanne. "Will you give me your wine at dinnertime?" she asked the girl. "They have stopped my ration."

"Mrs. Christie, if you please!" said the kind Irishwoman, Joan Beattie, and Mrs. Christie did then indeed quiet down to her cocoa.

The chaplain was slouching about behind them, watching. The mothers were soaking dry biscuit in cocoa and feeding their children from their own fingers. One woman was undoing her bodice to suckle her baby, her older child leaning his head against her side, and milk was dripping from her and Joan Beattie was saying, "Lydia, really, why do you let yourself get all filled up to the point of bursting like this? Just feed the babe when she is hungry." The chaplain let out a huff and turned his back.

"I do not wish to give those men up there any reason at all to think of me," said the woman. "I can wait until we are below, and so can the baby." She glanced irritatedly at a pair of young women whose voices had risen in their excitement at discovering they had once lived in the same street in Belfast. By them a slim little person was weeping softly, slowly unpinning her bonnet from her brown hair. The woman beside her, who Maryanne knew to be a gentle young countrywoman from Suffolk with three rosy children, began to stroke that brown hair. Maryanne thought, If only I could be unhappy in that manner, perhaps it would be better.

III.   That Scottish doctor who disapproved was a mushroomy man with a round white head and puffs of grey hair out each side, a big circle of a nose and a pair of cool pale eyes. "No, you may not bring her cocoa, young woman," he said to Maryanne standing there at the door to the little hospital, holding the pint cup, and she knew she had been wrong to try courage. "Go and take it away," he said, and there came a sickly swell that made them both plant their feet and brace for a moment, and the ship dropped in the sea and Sarah Ward off behind him moaned and vomited under the shifting light. Maryanne held the cup of cocoa steady. "Take it away and then come back with a bucket of water and a brush," he said.

The hospital was not a bad place, although it smelt badly. It adjoined their sleeping and eating place, but its shape was triangular, because it was situated at either the very front or the very end of the ship. She did not know which, because she grew disorientated belowdecks. It was small, but light. It had real square windows done in little grids and, besides these, a large lantern swaying on a chain which the doctor might light as he pleased. Besides these, there was also a hatch above, which only the doctor and officers were permitted to use, but which was left open to the sun and air on fine, calm days. There were six beds, with spindly legs bolted to the decking. There was a folding screen set around the bed farthest to the left, but Maryanne could see a pair of bare feet twisted in the blanket beyond it.

As Maryanne knelt by her maybe-friend's bed and got up the vomit from down between the boards as best she could, employing brush and water and fingernails, she thought it might be good to become a little sick, and that maybe that was why Sarah Ward did it. She looked up at her, but all she could see was a hank of red hair off the side of the bed and a white hand dangling. She touched the fingertips and then started, because on the forearm was a great round blister, larger than any she had seen, tight and round like a dewdrop seen from the perspective of an ant. But then she felt the doctor watching her and so she got back her task. If she took her time at it, she would not need to go back up and out amongst the women for a while. There was someone lumped up under the covers in another of the beds too, and a fourth bed was taken by the woman who never stopped being ill and might die, and Maryanne hoped that either person or the girl with the womb trouble behind the screen might vomit as well. But they were lying very still.

"That will do, Maginn," said the doctor, and so she went up on her heels and then stood. She did not know he knew her name. The doctor was looking at her there, looking with a critical eye. "How old are you?" he asked, and when she said she was fifteen, Sarah Ward, sick but listening, gave a moan of despair that she had not said she was twenty-one as they had agreed. But I did not agree, Maryanne wanted to say, and anyway, the doctor will have it all written down, and can check, and we will get thrown in the coal hole for lying.

"You speak well," said the doctor.

"Thank you, sir," she whispered.

"Have you an education?"

"Somewhat, yes, sir."

"In order to do something toward defeating the idleness that so pervades your ranks, I have decided to employ some of the women who are educated to a degree as governesses, so the others might at least read their Bibles, and although you are so young and meek they would mostly tear you in pieces, perhaps you can assist," he was saying to her, but she stopped listening, because the mention of governesses made her think of her mother, or, at least, the mother of the girl with the French name, and so all she could think of then was, again: Water, water. Water, water, water, water, everywhere, water.

"Are you stupid?" asked the doctor, mildly enough.

"I don't know, sir," she said, which was probably a stupid answer, and then, perhaps even stupider, standing there with vomit under her fingernails, the girl asked the doctor for a favour. "May I sit with Sarah Ward?" she asked.

He was so surprised he told her he had a daughter her age, and then he told her she must get rid of the slop in the bucket. And then he lectured her for some time about Edinburgh, which he said was a desirable place to live with a fine old castle and quite a milder climate than many might expect. And then he complained a while that it was most inappropriate that he had no nurse to assist him. And then he told her that Sarah Ward was a wicked girl and she, Maryanne, ought to talk to her about God and the Angels and at the same time close her ears to anything Sarah Ward might contribute to the discourse. And in fact, at another time she ought to borrow a Bible and read it aloud to her. Old Testament. And finally, he told her yes, very well, she might return after she had disposed of the vomit water, if she had no other duties awaiting her and if she washed her hands with soap, including under the fingernails, which seemed overly fastidious to her, but something she could do regardless.

Sarah Ward expressed her sadness in such terrible ways that Maryanne could not even speak when she returned from disposing of the vomit, could do nothing but put a hand against Sarah's wet forehead for a moment, and sit on the little stool beside her, tightening her body against the swell. The doctor was gone, so she did not have to talk about God and the Angels.

"Oh, Sarah," said Maryanne. "Why do you hurt yourself?"

"Tell me a story," said Sarah Ward, her voice like catgut, her face bone white and annoyed. "If you are so educated."

"I am not so educated. Sarah, how did you make this terrible blister?" she said, peering again at the straining blister on her forearm. Sarah Ward frowned.

"Do you not know medicine when you see it?" she asked. "It is his doing—look," she said, and pulled her shift down to show Maryanne another great blister upon her chest, between her breasts, and showed her other arm with the same. "My legs too," she said. "It does burn when he puts them on, but I don't mind a little burning. He is drawing out—well, I do not know what, exactly. Something bad. Now tell me a story."

Maryanne stared a moment, then collected herself. "I do not know any stories at all."

"Oh, yes, you do. Tell me about something."

"Sarah," said Maryanne again. "Did one of the sailors get at you? Are you—you know—?"

"You are a silly girl," Sarah said, but her cracked mouth was wry. "No, a sailor has not got at me yet. There is one I would not mind, you know. It is that tall one with the brown skin. I think he is from Devon."

"He is from Cornwall," said Maryanne, and Sarah looked sharp.

"How do you know?" she asked, and Maryanne could not find the words to say that he had told her but that she had not invited the telling. "I did not know I had a rival," said Sarah at last.

"I should rather hang myself," said Maryanne, quick and hot. "Truly, I should rather die."

"So should we all, I suppose," said Sarah, watching her. "I am tired of speaking now. Tell me a story to make it up to me."

Maryanne put her hands slowly over her face and held them there a moment, breathing in the fat from the soap she had used. "There was once a family," she said, and Sarah Ward told her to speak up and take her hands off her face. "There was once a family with a cook," Maryanne said again, folding her hands in her lap, "and the cook made them rice pudding for their supper. The next day, the girl of the family was playing in the garden when she saw a snake. The cook was also in the garden, picking apples for apple dumplings, and when she heard the girl scream, she dropped the apples everywhere and ran over lolloping like a great hound and took up the snake by its tail and whipped it against the wall until it was dead. Then she took it inside with the girl and cut open the belly of the snake and found inside a little brown mouse. And so they cut open the little brown mouse, and inside the mouse's belly were a few grains of rice pudding."

"What?" said Sarah.

But the lump in the second bed said, "Yes, very good," and then she rolled onto her back, long dark plait unweaving from the covers, profile fine in the warm light, and began to regale them. "The thing that is truly comforting about a story is that it possesses deliberate meaning," she said, in a voice most refined. "It has a nice little moral, or is an allegory, or, at the very least, is *about* something. This is not so in life, which is of course meaningless. One cannot, for example, think of one's home, and the last time that one saw it, or any of the times before that, and understand it all, and how it is complete, and thus have done. As it is, Maginn has told us a nice little story, which stands as an entire world unto itself. We have the apple tree and the snake and the girl in the garden. Quite classically done, my dear, and we yawn our way contentedly through all such symbols and are quite satisfied by the end where the rice pudding in the mouse reminds us of the beginning of the story and so makes a circle. But if the story were not a story, but a moment in a life, then it would not have ended there. The carcasses of the snake and mouse would have had to be done away with, burnt, perhaps, or buried, and meanwhile there would be happenings upstairs and in the laneway and in the neighbours' houses and also in Egypt and so on, and then perhaps someone—girl or cook—would have been scolded, and then the cook would have made her apple dumplings, and the family eaten them, and so on and on, for years, for all of time, in fact. Do you see? Meaningless."

Sarah Ward scoffed. "All right, Lady Muck," she said.

In the third bed, the woman who was always ill remained motionless, nothing but dank brown curls visible above the blanket.

"Has he asked you to be a governess yet?" Maryanne asked Lady Muck, but then Sarah Ward beside her winced and brought her knees up against her belly under the covers as the last of the colour went from her face.

"Maryanne—"

"I am here," Maryanne said, leaning in, and tried to stroke her hair as she had seen that gentle young woman from Suffolk do, but the red hair felt dense and unyielding, and she took her hand away again. Sarah shuddered, head to toe, and gave a sharp groan.

"You smell of sour milk," she whispered, eyes closed.

"I presume you are the girl in the story?" asked Lady Muck, languid, but Maryanne was saved from responding by the doctor's return.

"Out, Maginn!" he cried, shouldering the door open, carrying something in, a woman coming after him. It was the woman who also had all the milk coming out of her who had not wanted the sailors to see, and she had her hands up over her bonnet and then brought them down to press at her breast. Maryanne stood.

"Sir, doctor, Sarah Ward has taken a turn …" she said.

"Out!" he shouted at her again. "Out! Out!" And he brought the parcel he was carrying over to the bed beside Sarah Ward's and from it unwrapped the woman's baby. The mother was beginning to say some words in a high and strangled voice. Maryanne looked again at Sarah Ward, curled into herself, her face into the pillow. Maryanne's breasts prickled with milk of her own once more, and her arms began their ache.

"And you—Piper—out with you too. There is no need for you to be lying there." The bare feet behind the screen were pulled out of sight, and the doctor left the baby and went to push the screen to the side. It thumped and fell against a bulkhead. "Get dressed and go out," he said. "I have done all I can for you." The girl, hunched and white, rolled off the bed and began to pick at her stockings lying by her boots on the deck.

"Woman! You—Fernsby! Fetch me the cantharides powder, quickly now," said the doctor, over his shoulder, to the woman in bed who had ideas about life. "It is in the drawer, there. In the cabinet."

"I can fetch it," said Maryanne, lingering by Sarah Ward's bed, but no one minded her. The mother was saying no, no, no blisters, you will burn her, and no one minded her, either.

"You had better go," said Lady Muck, whose name was Fernsby, sitting up, elegant, calm, her dark plait over her shoulder, swinging her stocking feet off the side of her bed. "I shall attend this matter."

"I do not wish to leave Sarah Ward," she said, but Fernsby waved her off.

"There is nothing you might do for her," she said. "You are in the way." And so there was nothing else for Maryanne to do but go, but she took with her the image of Sarah Ward and her red hair wedged into the muscle of her heart. The girl with the womb trouble limped after.

In the place where they ate and slept there were some women standing together, talking in low voices, and they looked up at her when she came in. "Did you see anything? What is happening?" asked one.

"I do not know," said Maryanne, looking around for the girl with the womb trouble, but she hobbled past and through the open barred door and set herself to clambering painfully up the ladder. "Sarah Ward is ill and so is that baby. He said blistering."

"Well, she must not allow that," said one of the women. "That is a terrible practice upon a child."

"Blistering cured me of my cough," said Joan Beattie.

"But you are not a new baby, Joan," replied the other.

"That is true. A baby's skin is so very fine," said Joan, rubbing the tips of her fingers together as if testing the quality of silk. "It did burn," she added, ruminatively.

The skirt of one of the women was bunched. "Come now," that woman said, bending down and lifting a small child from behind her. The child held tightly to the rough fabric, and the others had to gently pull it from his hands and smooth it down. "Mama will return soon," the woman said to the boy. And then, to Maryanne, "How was Lydia?"

She hesitated, but then asked, "Who is Lydia?" and the woman tutted.

"Why, the mother, of course! The mother of the baby."

"She was upset," said Maryanne. "I think she said no blisters for the baby." The women nodded.

"Yes, you see? That is what I would say too," said one.

The chaplain's legs and then backside appeared beyond the doorway as he gingerly picked his way down. The woman with the child checked her skirt, checked the others had smoothed it down properly and no underthings were showing. The chaplain ducked in through the low door.

"What news?" the chaplain said. "They tell me the Sculthorpe infant has taken ill?"

"Yes, sir. She knows," said the woman holding the child, indicating Maryanne. The chaplain looked at her. He was an unhealthy-looking man, skinny, like a bellows had been put to his mouth and opened, and all the material of him sucked out, leaving only a gawky husk. He had large eyes that had survived the sucking, perfectly circular, and hair that might be faded with age or might simply be an undistinguished yellow-brown.

"Yes?" he said.

"I do not know anything, sir," said Maryanne. "Except that the baby is being seen by the doctor and its mother is there with it and Sarah Ward has taken a dreadful turn." Her voice went high, and the chaplain frowned.

"How old are you, girl?" he asked, but Maryanne did not wish to betray Sarah Ward again by not saying that she was twenty-one, and so she said nothing at all. "Well?" said the chaplain. "Speak!"

"Oh, leave her," said the woman holding the child. "She is just a mousy little girl."

"I pray you remember yourself, woman!" the chaplain said, offended, ineffectual. "It is not for you to tell me to whom I might speak!" But he looked at Maryanne and, indeed, had nothing more to say to her at that time, and went away back through the door and up the ladder and out the hatch above.

IV. After the chaplain had gone, the girl climbed carefully after him, away from the women who had directed their collective attention to her and expected her to understand something previously unspoken. She emerged into the bright clear air above bringing with her the restless feeling that she had left something behind, or left some important duty undone. It was Sarah Ward, of course, Sarah Ward there in her bed, white as the sheets, terrible blisters on her body, her hair gone garish red against her pallor.

The women were in their flocks again, seated together here and there. The girl with the womb trouble had curled herself up like a wounded cat on the deck near some matronly types who did not pay her any attention. Some women were picking at coarse stuff with needle and thread, and some others had their fingertips slipped into little books to mark their pages while they talked. Maryanne had no such pastime, and looked about, and found another of her little corners where she might go unnoticed. On her way there the ship dipped low and she darted sideways and gripped the rail for support. Despite this sudden buckling, the ocean was still entirely motionless to look at, like a great spill on the glassblower's floor that had been left to harden.

Others of the women cried quite often, but she had felt tears an impossibility, as if they had been shocked out of her at the moment of her creation as Maryanne Maginn. But now, looking again out at the desert of water, she found she had to tighten her mouth and throat and heart like fists inside her body against weeping. She stood there forcing the tears away.

The ship was their shelter, the small chalice carrying them through that which was inhospitable to human life. But there was no shelter for her there, she thought. There was only a series of confines between which she might move but never escape.

She understood this to be a moment of danger, when sadness and idleness might together unfix her from her present moment, from the all-that-there-is of the ship, and spin her backward into those memories she could not entertain, not for the sake of her sanity, or spin her forward into anticipation of what was to come, which was to be a terror, most likely. Such moments of danger would occur, of course. So now she did what she always did when her mind threatened her, which was to begin to think with great specificity of other things. What exactly this entailed depended on how she was occupied; at times she would count the back-and-forth of her scrubbing, or try to imagine the ship painted in different colours, or look at woman after woman and try to remember their names. Now, however, for lack of anything else, she began to tap her fingers. First twice, then four times, then eight, then sixteen, and she might have carried on into numbers so large they became mere abstractions when she was saved by the one who wished to save.

The chaplain had evidently thought of something to say to her, because he edged up to her right and placed one large-knuckled hand on the side, not far enough from hers for her liking. The way he had his hand on the rail meant his body was turned toward her and his left hand was unaccounted for, behind her. She dropped her eyes from the glass ocean to stare at her hands gripping the wood and his there beside them.

"Maryanne, child," he said, softly, long toothed and sincere. "Every wise woman *buildeth* her house, but the foolish *plucketh* it down with her hands. Yes?"

"Yes, sir," she murmured, and the stupidity of it was the thing that finally quashed the urge to weep and to remember. A calm came over her. The chaplain repeated his words, more slowly.

"Every wise woman buildeth her house. But the foolish plucketh it down," he said. "What do you make of it?"

Maryanne paused. "I think it very true," she said, and he nodded beside her.

"Now, it is not really about the building of houses, is it?" he asked her.

"No, sir, I suppose it is not," she said.

"What wisdom do you take from this?"

"I do not know, sir," she said, humbly, and he smiled and looked out to sea.

"A wise woman … what does a wise woman do?"

"Buildeth her house," she said, and the chaplain smiled again.

"Yes," he said, patiently, "but what is the meaning of it?"

Maryanne wrung her hands on the railing. She wished to let go; his hand was too close, but then she was afraid she would stumble against him if the movement of the ship surprised her. "Well, sir, I suppose a wise woman creates, and a foolish woman destroys. But surely that is true of anybody," she said. The chaplain looked a little surprised.

"Yes," he said, and then, for the second time that morning, he found himself with nothing more to say to her, and he patted the ship's railing twice, and she felt his left hand hovering over her back, but he sidled away without going so far as to touch her. Maryanne set her teeth. He was an idiot man; the proverb was about a wife, surely, and her husband and children, and how she was to care for her family and her home, and was therefore not relevant. He ought to have brought her the one about blessed is she that believes, or, no, better, the one about lowliness and meekness. Then a thought struck her.

"Sir?" she called after him, and he turned with a look of eagerness on his face. She kept her own face low as she said, "I think that girl might need some help."

"Which girl?"

"The one—you know, sir, the one who had a little trouble this morning." He reddened, and his eagerness fell away.

"Women's troubles are for the women. Now, you remember what we have discussed," he said, and left.

She closed her eyes a moment, and then continued to her obscure corner to tuck herself away until dinnertime.

Her corner gave her a good view of the hatch, and she watched as Lydia Sculthorpe's little boy was helped up and over by the women coming up behind him, and last of all was the kind Irishwoman Joan Beattie. She watched as this woman went to the crate of their bedding and wrestled out a straw mattress and a blanket and dragged them toward the hatch. The little boy Sculthorpe had been standing quite lost and now came and picked up a trailing corner of the blanket and followed after her with it. Joan smiled back at him, and then, glancing into the hatch, she had him help her push the bedding in, which was really no help at all, so tiny was he, and then she climbed down after. He tried to go with her, but she said something to the other women, and they took him away. His eyes were like copper pennies.

The girl set herself to think of what she would think of, which would probably be Sarah Ward, although she did not know how to think of her without fear. And then that great rose of a woman Fernsby from the hospital put her head up from below and climbed into the air, looking around, and seeing her. She had her dark hair tucked under her bonnet and was firmly done up in her mean clothing as they all must be, but she strolled like a lady at a garden party.

"Oh, Maginn, my dear," she said. "The doctor has found me to be a very poor nurse and has asked for you instead." Maryanne looked up at her. The sun was behind her, and her form was darkened. There was a flash, and Maryanne glanced over to see an officer had come to watch, brass buttoned and cool. Fernsby gave no sign of seeing him. "Come, dear," she said, and waited while Maryanne got to her feet. "He seems to think you shall do as you are told."

Maryanne nodded. "Yes, I shall."

"Oh, no, Maginn! You must not," said Fernsby, stooping a little to speak softly to her as they picked their way carefully back to the hatch. "If the mother does not wish the doctor to blister the baby, or bleed her, or do any such cruelty, you must add your voice to hers and help her prevent him."

"That is difficult," said Maryanne.

"Not at all," said Fernsby.

"But the doctor must know …"

"Blistering will not help the baby," said Fernsby. "Any fool knows that you must not break the skin of a child. If he were a mother, he would know. I was bled once as a small child," she added. "It was not therapeutic. My mother always maintained it nearly killed me and I recovered despite it. And blistering is surely worse, for the pain is worse."

In another life, perhaps Maryanne would have been good enough to brush Fernsby's hair and sit on a low stuffed stool by her chair by the fire and read to her, and call her Miss or Madam, depending. She couldn't have been so great a lady, of course, given the circumstances. Or perhaps she had been, and none of the men in her family wanted to pay for her anymore.

"It is the easiest thing in the world to do what is right, and hang the consequences," Fernsby told her. "Believe you me, you should prefer to be cast down in the coal hole for a day or two knowing you have acted properly than to be sitting comfortably about, a traitor. The latter is very bad for the spirit," she said, and left her to go back down into the dark mouth of the hatch alone.

v. The berth she shared with Sarah Ward and two others was one of the less amenable, situated in the middle, far from either hatch. There the air lay sullen and thin, seeping in through the air scuttles high up in the bulkhead, too high to be of much use. The berths were built one above the other, and theirs was a lower. In the daytime the berths were nothing but wooden frames, with the bedding up on deck to air, partly for hygiene and partly so the women could not hide anything devious beneath their mattresses. Now, however, when Maryanne picked her way down the ladder and through the low labyrinthine room, she found Joan Beattie had taken the bedding for their own berth, and that Sarah Ward was lying there, clothed and bonneted. Joan was kneeling beside her, and she looked up at Maryanne coming cautiously toward them. "Did Miss Fernsby find you?" asked Joan.

"Yes, she did."

Joan sighed and looked down at Sarah Ward. "The doctor would not allow Sarah to stay," she said softly. "I do not think he cares for her. He has allowed that other woman to remain—the one who has been ill from the first day—and she has a temper, as I discovered when I tried to take her bedding to wash. But not Sarah." She shook her head. "It hurt her to move her. You little girls! Why are you here? You ought to be at home with your mothers," she said, and then, "If I were a mother my heart should just about tear out of my chest." Maryanne came to kneel at Sarah Ward's other side, but Joan shook her head. "He wants you to help with the baby. You had best go."

Sarah lay stiffly, her skin grey. The only indication Maryanne could see that she was not dead was the tension in her, the tightness with which her eyes were closed and the quivering lines of her body. Maryanne came a little closer, wanting to look at Sarah's throat, maybe, or more closely at her face, but Joan Beattie said, "Go!" and so she skittered off to the hospital to do as she was told, except for when she mustn't.

The air in the hospital was closer than before, and Sarah Ward's bed was yet unmade, although the one where Fernsby had been lying was tucked tight and smooth. The curly head of the woman who was always sick and might die was still there, her face and body hidden beneath the blanket. The mother, Lydia Sculthorpe, was standing leaning against a bulkhead, her hands now at her throat, watching, horrified, as the doctor peered over her baby. He looked up at Maryanne and came over to take her elbow and guide her away. She felt a shock at being touched by him, his hand large and foreign, but he did it casually, like he was moving some small item to a position more convenient. "Maginn," he said. "The baby is ill. I must administer a blister to each leg. You can read, can you not, and you have a steady hand? You can comprehend and carry out a direction if I give it to you?"

"Yes, sir," she said.

"Sculthorpe," said the doctor, to the mother. "Maginn will assist in the application of the blister powder."

"No," the mother said, rushing to the bed and standing over her baby as if to ward him off. "No, Doctor, you will not wear me down, sir. You cannot do that to her."

"Foolish!" he cried, slapping the bulkhead by Maryanne's shoulder, making her wince. He pointed a thick grey fungus of a finger at Lydia Sculthorpe. "My patience is continually tested! You mark my words: If that infant dies, it will be not from illness, but from your inanity, and the conspiracy of women." He strode off to a tall desk and opened a brown journal there, leafing through it, and, finding his page, ran his finger down a column, and then began to take some brisk notes with a fine gold pen. Maryanne moved quietly over to Lydia Sculthorpe and her baby.

"What is the baby's name?" she whispered.

"Mary," Lydia Sculthorpe whispered back. "Have you seen my little lad? Are they taking care of him?"

"Yes, they are … he is abovedecks with them now."

"What are you whispering about?" asked the doctor, his voice clipped.

"We are praying, sir," spat Lydia Sculthorpe, and the doctor glanced back at them a moment. "He does not know that we are human beings," she said to Maryanne, dropping her voice once more as he turned away. "He does not know *she* is a human being." And she kissed the baby's head, and then bunched the blanket in her hands so violently her knuckles went white.

"Maginn, will you discover the name of the infant, for my notes," said the doctor flatly, still writing.

"She is called Mary Sculthorpe, sir," answered Maryanne.

"How do you know?" he asked, pausing in his writing and turning to look at her again.

"I asked, sir."

He looked at her a moment longer, and then turned back to his notes. "Mary Sculthorpe," he said, writing, and then, "Age?"

"Three months," said Lydia Sculthorpe, and the doctor stood still, his back yet to them, and they both understood at once that they were waiting for Maryanne to repeat this information, for he had decided like a churlish schoolboy not to listen to Lydia.

"Three months," said Maryanne, and he wrote this down with a flourish.

"Fernsby took it upon herself to put the cantharides powder away," he said. "Fetch it from the drawer." He briskly indicated a cabinet on the flat wall by the door. "Can—tha—rides," he repeated. "C—A—N—and so forth." Maryanne glanced at Lydia Sculthorpe and her baby again, and then went over. The cabinet was a sturdy item of dark wood, bolted to the floor and walls. She opened the doors and sighed a little at the many fussy drawers within, each marked with a card written with fresh ink. The drawer marked *Cantharides* was right in the middle, right before her eyes. She began opening drawers, other drawers, to packets and tins and bundles of linen, and closing them again.

"What are you doing?" he asked her, and she looked back at him watching her, carefully closing both lids on his travel inkwell, and so she opened the correct drawer, and took out a little tin. She glanced over at the windows, which did not open, of course, and at Lydia Sculthorpe leaning on the bed with her arms lightly about her baby, and she took the cap off the tin and poured the entirety of the brown powder into her own left palm. Then, holding this powder carefully, she put the tin and its cap back in the drawer with her right hand, and closed the drawer, and the cabinet doors, and then brought her right hand down and began rubbing the blister-powder between her palms and quite thoroughly over her fingers too. She let the great excess of it drift to her skirt and the floor, and although the doctor overcame his shock and lurched toward her, the burning had already begun.

VI. She knew herself to be underwater. Although she could breathe, it was a cautious breathing, as though her air might be stopped at any time. The creak of the ship was different down here; it was more of an act of resistance than the simple shifting and settling of abovedecks. The officer led Maryanne, while Peter Rowe the Cornish sailor quietly followed with a lantern. The officer bent fluidly, unbolted the hatch at his feet, and swung it open. A hot light arose from below.

"Go down," said the officer, so she went, backward, quiet. Her hands in their wrapped linen bandage smarted against the wooden rungs, and the thick glass bottle of water that hung on a cord about her neck swung awkwardly. She descended into a place of oily light, rich with golden and dark wood, planks stacked high and curls of it like autumn leaves beneath her feet. The walls and low ceiling were tacked with tools in firm brackets, and a large bench under an overhang was so crowded with these tools and pieces of wood that she did not at first see the carpenter himself gnomed up under there, over his work, three lanterns ablaze, until he pushed something away from him and turned to watch them come. His eyes sparked under a low and shining brow. He asked her something, but he spoke so low and fast she could not understand him. Peter Rowe shook his head and the carpenter, smiling a little, ducked back down to his labours. The officer cleared his throat, but the exchange had passed him by, apparently, because when he spoke it was to ask her about Fernsby.

"What is her name?" he asked. "Her Christian name?"

"I do not know, sir," said Maryanne.

"Hmm." He brought her over to another hatch, sweeping it of wood shavings with his boot, and stooping to unbolt and swing it open. "Go down," he said, again, but this time the hole was dark, and Peter Rowe held the lantern out over the hatch that she might see the ladder. She stood for a moment, but then crouched and took herself backward and down into a small and tarry hold filled with bundled rope of all sizes. The officer and then Peter Rowe came down after her, although there was so little room to stand that Peter Rowe remained hanging on the ladder in order to hold the lantern above them. She checked her bottle; the cork was firmly in place, the water right up to it. She had the thought of escaping up and up into the open air to perhaps throw herself into the ocean, but the hard glass of the water she had seen would surely not yield to her anyway.

"The carpenter ought to have natural light," mused the officer, apparently to Peter Rowe, who said,

"Aye, sir."

"I shall mention it to the captain."

The smell in the little hold was dense with the mustiness of tar. The groans of the ship were like those of an injured animal, but far away, and muffled. "Step aside," said the officer, and she saw that there was another hatch below her feet. "This is the final one," he said, as she shuffled back against the bundles of rope, and the officer bent to unfasten the bolt and swing the hatch open. She looked up in this moment, to delay witnessing the place she was to go. Looking up meant looking at Peter Rowe, but the lantern was between them and so all she had was his silhouette. So she looked down. There was another ladder and another well of black, but the lantern did not dispel it. "Go down," the officer told her, and she took a breath, and went and knelt by the ladder and dropped her legs backward in to begin her final descent. The cold of it welled up at her. The room with the ropes was warm, but down below was a deep and inhuman iciness. She looked back up at Peter Rowe, who did not leer at her, and who had once asked her name. Now that her position had shifted she could see his face, although she could not read his expression.

"Bear up," he said, holding the light out and down. "Go elsewhere in your mind. Whatever place you have in there that is pleasant." Maryanne thought the officer might not like his talking to her, but the officer in his brass buttons was scarcely paying attention, his hands in his pockets, gazing ruminatively at the rope as he waited.

"A fine woman," he mused. "Remarkable that she is amongst your kind."

"I cannot do it," said Maryanne, hearing the scurrying of rats below. The shift of the boat tried to pull her from the ladder so forcefully that she clung to it, not moving.

"Come, girl," said the officer, shaking his head not in disapproval but to clear it of his daydreaming, it seemed. "I must get back. They told me you destroyed medicine with which the doctor was to treat an infant child. Go down and take your punishment, for you may find you are the better for it when you come back up again."

"May I keep the light?" she asked, still clinging to the ladder.

"What! No! You would set the entire ship on fire," said the officer. "Go down, now, and no more silliness. Many have gone down before you and arisen again well chastened."

And so she went, hand below hand, looking up at Peter Rowe bearing the light above until she set her feet on the coal which rattled and shifted and she sank nearly to her knees. The officer flipped the hatch shut and all light was extinguished with such suddenness and extremity her eyes smarted. The drawing of the bolt was a low, slow grating, and then she heard the voice of the officer ordering Peter Rowe back up, and there were no more sounds from above. She breathed a deep and trembling breath, tasting coal dust, feeling it in her throat.

"Shall I be forgotten or remembered?" she asked the air.

She stood holding the ladder for some time in that perfect blackness, perfect freezing solitude, until she shifted the coal and let her knees find the floor. She knelt leaning against the rungs of the ladder, all her legs pressed in by hard-edged coal, uncomfortable but anchored. She shut her eyes as if she might fool herself the darkness was her own doing. She kept still there, except that she kicked her feet from time to time to keep the rats away. And to remind herself that she could indeed move, and was not half buried alive.

First she became very distracted by the idea that she was still wearing Joan Beattie's shawl. She ought to have given it back, she chided herself, before being taken below. But truly she was glad to have it for the warmth, and for the smell of sheep, which gave her hope that somewhere out there in the world there were still green fields. But that comfort did also bring a bitterness, because it necessarily reminded her that someone had been kind to her, and had performed for her an act of care of which she was probably not worthy, which was almost too much for her to think about. And so she made herself stop worrying about the shawl, which also took away the green fields. And that left her there in the blackness. So then she began to revisit the moment in the hospital when she had poured out the blister dust. She ought to have pretended to stumble, and dropped it, and then maybe she would not be here now.

She thought of Joan Beattie talking about how young she and Sarah Ward were, how they ought to be with their mothers, but before that thought could betray her into a yearning for the mother of the dead girl with the French name, she felt something tug at her skirt. It was minute but undeniable, and she shrieked and grappled with the ladder, not knowing which way was climbing and which way was falling, scrabbling, coal dust thickening, until finally she managed to bring herself up off the deck to hang on the rungs as Peter Rowe had with the lantern. She was afraid somehow in her confusion she had uncorked the bottle, maybe, or damaged it, but when she took it in her hands it was cold and smooth and replete, the cork still in place.

Rats can climb better than you can, she thought, and then, Do not think of it.

Her heart was beating so fast and loud that she was afraid she would not hear the scurryings of the rats again and would not know if they came close. She did not know how to quiet her heart, so she began to sing the one song she could recall in that moment to distract herself. It was "Early One Morning," which was a pretty tune but had been sung too often by the women after their dinner when they were feeling ruminative, or abovedecks in the sunset when the chaplain was busy off saving some girl or other, until they had been told to sing something else because the captain was growing irritated. Maryanne could not recall all the words, and so sang the first few lines over and over, either for minutes or hours, until her mouth was dry. And then there she was again, in the blackness.

She wanted water badly, but didn't dare, in case she became confused once more and spilt the lot of it. Her heart had quietened, now, and so she listened again for rats, and she heard them too, scratching and rustling. Then she came to understand she could hear something else as well, and her heart quickened once more, and she felt a kind of plunging in her soul. The creaking of the ship had been masking it, perhaps, but now all at once it was perfectly clear. She first told herself it was rats, and then ropes, but then she could think of nothing else it might be but a baby crying, and she knew it had been crying for some time, perhaps even the entire time. It was Lydia Sculthorpe's baby, of course, and the crying was not a bad sign, for crying was a sign of life, and lungs that would fill with air. The trouble with this idea was that the crying was coming from down, somewhere, below her feet. Her breasts began to prickle with milk and that aching came into her arms again and she knew and had always known it to be the ache of emptiness, the ache of a particular absence, and she gasped in a great breath and let go of the ladder and dropped down into the coal, twisting her foot, banging her shoulder, scraping her face, and scrabbling around to find her own little lost baby whose cries were growing worse and worse.

    Her heart was going fast again, but even the banging of it and the tumbling of the coal and her own shrieks could do nothing to drown out the crying. But wherever she moved her hands there was only coal, or wood. Once she touched a warm body but it was furry and it darted away. She dived after it and banged into a bulkhead, or perhaps the deck, or the ladder, or something, and the bottle around her neck clacked and cracked and cold water soaked right through the shawl and her bodice and shift and slapped against her skin. Now there was broken glass too, and a broken bottleneck about her own neck, but she continued flailing around, calling out, scratching and crawling, and the crying went on, always below, always beyond, until she banged again into something, hard, on her head, and for the first time down there she saw a flash of light, but it was only for an instant.

    The crying was gone, like a mouse into a snake's mouth.

For a confusing time, she thought she was home. Truly home, in the place she had decided she would not remember, where the light was soft through curtains. Her mother sat by her bed and talked to her until she fell asleep. Never stories, but terrible, dry things, like how to decline various verbs in Latin or French, or how to go about growing a flower garden, or how to make bobbin lace. So she lay in her bed and her mother sat by and filled that dizzy silence with talk.

    "In order to make a lace collar, you will need certain items," she said. "One, many silk threads. Two, a set of bobbins. Three, a straw-filled cushion. Four, a piece of card. Five, many pins. Now, there are three kinds of lace you may make with bobbins. The first is straight lace, in which the lace-maker might employ a great number of bobbins in order to produce lace in one piece. Next, we come to part lace. Part lace is an amusing method of making lace with the help of a friend, for it is worked in pieces and later joined in a manner I shall latterly describe. Finally, we have braid lace. Braid lace uses fewer bobbins than its two counterparts and is thus more economical." The girl lay listening to her mother with the glowing curtains drawn against the hush of early twilight in the village and she blinked softly and was then in bed in the hospital, and she felt many hours or perhaps days had passed, but she could not account for them. She looked over and saw the curly head of the woman who was always ill bundled with the covers all over the rest of her. This woman slowly uncurled and rolled onto her back, and the girl could see the great mound of her pregnant belly below the blankets.

It hurt to move her head. Her hands hurt too, and her ankle, and elsewhere. Then she closed her eyes and she fell asleep again. When next she woke up she thought to turn her sore head the other way and look for Lydia Sculthorpe and her baby, but they were not there. She was terribly thirsty, and she remembered the black hole and the crying in it, and tried to push herself out of bed, so that she could go back down there and look again, maybe with a lantern, this time. Maybe with Peter Rowe to help her. But the act of sitting upright made her spurt vomit directly across the bedclothes. Someone with soft hands brought water to her lips, and she drank and then fell asleep again. The next time she woke up she thought of the black hole once again, but this time her head felt clearer and she understood there was nothing down there other than rats and coal, and so she lay still, waiting for what would next be done.

VII. "There is an entire sky out there," said Sarah Ward, musingly, looking out the little squares of the windows behind the beds. Maryanne gazed and gazed at her, too sore to move. She could not see the windows, but it felt like it was nighttime. The lantern above swayed golden, the light sliding back and forth over Sarah, pulling at the shadows of her face. Her white cap framed her face sweetly, softening the sharpness, red hair wisping out. She looked thin, and a little tired.

"What?" Sarah snapped. "What are you looking at?"

"Are you alive?"

"Oh, lord, yes," said Sarah. "I will never die. I am a spirit."

"Is that true?"

"Yes! What—do you think a spirit would lie?"

"I suppose not."

"No! I am an undying spirit, and sometimes I need to try and get as close to death as I can so that I might understand what you mere mortals must face. Otherwise I could not live amongst you. I would be too lofty."

A terrible pressure came away from Maryanne's body and she felt so light she might rise from the bed.

"That girl Mary Piper with the womb trouble is sick, but she does not want us to tell the doctor," said Sarah Ward.

"Why not?"

"Why do you think? You know where her trouble is! She does not want his hands up there again."

"That is fair," said Maryanne, dreamily. "I am in your place, and you in mine," she added, the warm light dipping and sliding.

"Do you mean you were sitting here while I was lying where you are? Yes. This stool is a fright," said Sarah, wiggling. "How did you sit so straight? Damn it. I hate a seat without a back." She stood abruptly and pushed Maryanne's legs aside so she could half recline on the narrow bed, leaning heavily on her. It hurt, and was good. "This is scarcely better," she said. "For a little thing, you take up a good deal of room. Why do we not get chairs?"

"Because we do not deserve them," said Maryanne.

"Yes. We are too foul for chairs."

"Yes."

"Chairs are for the purehearted."

"Yes." They smiled at one another, and Maryanne felt her lips crack.

"You look as if you have lost a fight with a tiger," said Sarah.

"Perhaps I have."

"Oh, do not get poetic with me. I know you were wrestling yourself down in the coal hole."

"Am I filthy?" asked Maryanne.

"I should think so," said Sarah slyly, which Maryanne did not quite understand, although it made her blush.

"I mean do I have coal dust on me?"

"No. That Beattie woman washed you."

Maryanne nodded, and then, said, thick voiced, "I was afraid you would die."

"And that is why you were rolling around in the coal?"

"No—but I was afraid for you regardless."

Sarah waved a dismissive hand. It seemed too loose, like the flesh and veins and all the matter keeping her wrists together had been eaten away by the poison she had taken, leaving her hand to simply flap on a bare joint. "We have already addressed that matter. I am an undying spirit. Why were you at yourself down there?" But Maryanne could not find the words to say, and she watched as Sarah Ward grew bored above her. "Never mind," said Sarah, standing and stretching her fingertips high, and then brushing down the front of her dress. "I am not supposed to be in here, so I ought to creep back now and curl up next to our dear berthmates and dream of your friend the sailor from Cornwall. I need a sponge up my petticoats when I think of him or I get all greasy."

Maryanne needed to say something to keep her there. "That woman is pregnant," she said, desperately.

"Which one?"

"The one there, who will likely die." At this, the woman in the next bed with the chestnut hair groaned and rolled her bulk over.

"No," she said. "I will not die." Her eyes were as glazed and wide and unseeing as a pair of cracked eggs.

"Oh! Forgive me!" said Maryanne. "I did not know you were awake." Sarah Ward was laughing at her, but even as she laughed, she was casting around.

"Where is the water? None in here? That is poorly done of the doctor. I will go out to the dipper and get you some, but I will have to feel my way, so if I spill it you will have to go thirsty," she said, either to Maryanne or the other woman, or both, and was gone, and she must have spilt the water, Maryanne thought, because she did not return that night.

There was then a dream of sitting by a red fire set in a brick hearth. The flames swayed and snapped. She was on a worn jute rug, very plain and poor, but the room she was in was otherwise in complete darkness. The fire entranced her, flames flickering and darting like hot little tongues. But then from the room behind her a shuffling came, a shuffling toward her. It was a sound like somebody ailing in stiff silk and slippers. She could not turn around, and she felt the air on her neck begin to move, to whisper against her skin. She watched as slowly from the quiet darkness beside her came a pair of white hands holding open a great bellows. The hands moved forward and she saw the arms, the black sleeves, and then they stopped, so the face and body were hidden in the dark. There was a breathing and the hands tightened and squeezed the bellows down and a shining purple thing came ballooning from the end, larger and larger until it suckered away from the bellows and fell to sizzle wetly in the fire. The breathing grew louder and the hands continued to press the bellows down and out came a red thing like a birth, a bloody circle that fell. And then a long snake of more glistening purple and white went coiling into the fire. These things, these organs, were so wet and heavy that the fire started to go out.

When next she woke the doctor told her it was Sunday and she must get up and make her bed and dress properly and go up on deck for prayers. Lydia Sculthorpe was in the hospital again, lying with her baby in her arms. Maryanne floated, unfixed.

The wind had picked up and the sails snapped above them like clean sheets. The women knelt on the deck, the officers on chairs behind them. Sarah Ward darted her a quick look which was to say, See? *They* get chairs. Sailors stood behind those seated.

    The children were restless. Their mothers were trapped in constant movement, winding the little bodies over and over themselves.

    Maryanne's hands had barely blistered, for the cantharides powder had not had long enough to take such effect, but still they were pink and raw. Her neck was scratched and had come up in scabs, and her ankle was tender to walk upon. Her head ached, and ached more when she bent it to pray. The chaplain was intoning something irrelevant not only to them but to most of humanity. "For the priesthood being changed," he said, "there is made of necessity a change also of the law. For he of whom these things are spoken pertaineth to another tribe, of which no man gave attendance at the altar."

    Maryanne was praying that poem again, that Water, water. Water, water, everywhere. At least that could not be argued with when you were on a boat, and being correct brings a kind of satisfaction.

    Sarah Ward leant against her. "I am to help with the cooking this week," she whispered. "It is not yet my turn, but the doctor thinks I need honest occupation." Then, when Maryanne nodded tightly but did not reply, she continued, "He has decided we shan't be put down the coal hole anymore, after your great performance. He's going to have the carpenter build a special little box to lock us in, to be kept up on deck where we might be watched." A small boy beside her made a leap from his mother's arms and knocked her, and so she knocked into Maryanne, and they swayed together.

"Maginn!" said the chaplain, loud and sharp. "Silence!" The women kept their heads down.

"It was me, sir," said Sarah Ward, lifting her face to him. He did not know what to do with that act of honest fellowship, and so he hemmed and hawed and finally ignored it and read on. Sarah dropped her head again, but Maryanne saw her hidden smile.

A toddler sitting on her mother's lap lurched to the side and escaped, the mother and the women around grabbing for her. The child scrambled to Maryanne and launched herself at her. The mother stooped in, scooping the child, dipping herself to the chaplain. "I had better take her, sir …" she was saying, and the chaplain waved her off, and off she went, triumphant, it seemed, sending amused looks to her friends. She backed down the hatch, holding the girl over her shoulder. Meanwhile, the little Sculthorpe boy with eyes like copper pennies began to wail for his mother, and several other children cried because he was crying.

"Yes! Very well!" the chaplain cried, his voice rising and cracking to be heard. "All children must be taken below!"

There was murmuring from the officers behind them. The low women darted after their own children and wrestled them away, making their way backward down the hatch with little ones writhing over them. And so Maryanne and Sarah Ward and perhaps only half of the women remained to listen about many priests and the changing of laws thereunto.

"Sir, do we have souls?" asked Sarah Ward, right over the intonations of the chaplain. He looked up with a flash of malice, but again ignored her, and continued his reading. But the assuredness had gone from his voice. He stood before them, saying his words, his book wilting from his hands, impotent and wretched, but then even his words limped into silence when the gentle young countrywoman from Suffolk arose from below and asked if any of the women remaining above decks were midwives, because the one who might die was in labour. The old witch Mary Christie grunted and shuffled and creaked her body up.

"I am she," she said, and limped away and down with her limbs folded like an old bird.

VIII. At first it was the impulse of many to laugh at the cries winding out from behind the closed hospital door and throughout their quarters. It was laughter of the hard kind they had, although it was not cruel, exactly. Knowing, perhaps. But then the hours wore on, and they were not allowed back abovedecks and were not told why not, and the cries grew worse. And so the laughter died, and silence fell amongst the women, although the children grew irritable and wept often.

Lydia Sculthorpe crept out from the hospital and amongst them, her bodice all undone and her baby suckling. Her friends opened their arms to her and she went down couched amongst them. Her toddler son, who had been sleeping against someone's breast, moaned and wailed and tottered to collapse onto her other breast and went quiet again.

Mary Piper wandered to her berth and stood looking at it. Without its mattress and bedding, it offered nothing but hard planks. She stood before it, and then leant forward until her forehead was pressed against the berth above it. Finally, she folded her body down onto the planks and lay on her side with her knees up against her chest. "She is an odd girl," whispered someone.

With little talk, and no songs, the hours stretched like slow treacle. The birthing woman began to groan, deep and close, like some beast of the field in useless distress. Dinnertime crept upon them. Those who were food monitors leapt to their feet and were gone too long and returned with dragging feet and reluctant hands under their great trays of afternoon rations. The salt mutton was tougher even than usual and they were chewing and chewing as the woman lowed and groaned. They were given an extra ration of wine, even Maryanne, and Sarah Ward, whose wine rations had been stopped. Maryanne drank hers quick. Joan Beattie took some to Mary Piper curled up on the boards, but Mary would not drink. The plush, coarse young woman called Elizabeth Duncan whom the captain took for himself every night and sometimes in the day came down and whispered that even he could hear the screams from the hospital, all the way up above them. She looked frightened.

A particular feeling had come upon Maryanne. It was a feeling of rising up out of herself and looking back down at her own body very little and brittle and crabbed in agony. A feeling of something breaking most terribly, like perhaps a translucent porcelain dish put under such pressure it burst into dust. And an utter sense of abjection, of the inside come out.

They sat there drinking their wine, the silences welling deep and taut only to be broken by the beastlike calling from beyond the hospital door. The women who were cleaning monitors took their dishes and cups back into the large trays to take away and wash, and still nobody was saying much. A few were praying. The babies cried. Sarah Ward went primly to the water closet to vomit.

Finally the chaplain came and told them they might go above. In a flow like a white-capped river, everybody climbed into the golden air. Lydia Sculthorpe and her children went supported on either side by friends, and Mary Piper came shuffling behind.

Abovedecks, the sun spread like oil over the broad water. The ship was a trembling handful of sticks. The women were pinning themselves together now, pressed close in their muted circles. Lydia Sculthorpe sat like the Madonna holding her sickly baby, her head nodding, her son draped over her knee.

Maryanne sat close with Sarah Ward, Joan Beattie, Elizabeth Duncan whom the captain took, Mary Piper who was wet and dank with sweat, and two or three others. They were directly on the deck, knee to knee, shoulder to shoulder, warm and soft. Looking up at them, and around at the others, Maryanne saw a kind of vapour rising into the low golden air. Barely visible forces were exiting the dark of their bodies to hang about them and map themselves for all to see, so any one of them might glance at another or hear her name and gain immediate access to all kinds of information about her, about what she would think of some matter, what she would choose, and how she would feel. The girl called Maryanne saw this and knew it had always been there. A soft wing beat in her heart.

The sun fell softly and pooled their faces in shadow under their bonnets, but Joan Beattie lifted her face to it. She was wearing her brown shawl. It was clean. "Did I not dirty that?" asked Maryanne. "I did not mean to wear it down into the coal hole."

"I have washed it, my dear," said Joan Beattie. "I hope it gave you a little warmth."

A scream came distant from below.

"May I wear it?" whispered Mary Piper, and then cleared her throat, and said too loudly, "I am freezing cold." Her skin was red and glistening but she hugged her arms about herself, and Joan Beattie unwrapped herself and draped the shawl over the girl's shoulders.

"You really ought to go to the doctor," she said, but Mary shook her head tightly.

Elizabeth Duncan, fat on meat from the captain's table, asked Joan Beattie why she had never married.

"You shouldn't ask that," said a wan girl with a baby in each arm. She was red haired, like Sarah Ward, but her hair was limper and duller than Sarah's.

A woman languidly unfolded from a row on a bench against the far railing and strolled toward them; it was Fernsby, with her socialite's sense for gossip.

"She can ask," said Joan Beattie, and sighed, and moved herself sideways to allow Fernsby to rest herself down amongst them to listen. "We might as well talk. It is no great tragedy. Betsy Duncan here has asked me why I did not ever marry," she said to Fernsby.

"Good heavens," said Fernsby, civilly, and the birthing woman moaned up through the boards.

"I *was* to marry, in fact. When I was seventeen or eighteen I was engaged to a soldier who gave me a little ring with a stone in it," Joan Beattie said, drawing a small circle in the air as if to indicate the shape of the stone. "A little green stone. I liked him. But then my brother's wife—they lived in Liverpool—she died, and you know they had children, eight of them I think, no, nine, and she died having the tenth, so I had to go off from Ireland to Liverpool and live with my brother and care for the children and there was no room for the soldier, because then I would have had children of my own and it would have been too many, and I would not have been able to care for my nieces and nephews too, even if he had wanted to come to Liverpool with me. He was English, so perhaps he might have. But I didn't ask him to. And I suppose he didn't say it, either."

Their little circle was quiet a moment, but then Sarah Ward surprised Maryanne and perhaps all of them by saying, with some tenderness, "You'd have made a fine mother, Joan Beattie." Joan smiled, but then another cry came from below, and her smile slipped away, and she looked out at the water.

"It is a funny thing to feel, you know. I raised those children and loved them like my own, and yet here I am, alone."

"That is for the best," said Sarah Ward.

"What will they do with her if she dies? Or the baby?" whispered Elizabeth Duncan, and they shushed her. "Oh, I am forever saying the wrong thing!" she said, and crossed her arms tightly. "I am not wishing them dead!"

"They will put them over the side," said Joan Beattie.

"Into the water?"

"Yes."

There was another lull, and the girl felt them all listening and trying not to listen for cries from below, but there were none. "How deep is the sea?" she asked.

"Oh, fathoms and fathoms," said Joan.

"What is a fathom?" asked Elizabeth Duncan, but Sarah Ward talked a little over her to say instead,

"I hate it here. It's a *bad* fucking God *damned* place."

"Yes, my dear," said Joan, and placed a gentle hand on her knee, and then took it away again. "You know," she began, but she grew distracted by the sight of the mushroomy doctor emerging up from a hatch beyond their pen, and making his way to the grand door up there that had the captain's rooms somewhere behind it. The women all watched him go into the darkness of the doorway, his broad back blinking out like a tired eye.

"What?" said Sarah Ward.

"What?" said Joan Beattie.

"You were going to tell us something more."

Joan shifted her weight, easing her legs from under her. "Yes," she said. "Goodness me, this kneeling does my knees no favours!" she added. "I suppose the doctor has left the women's business to the women." The girl with the twins nodded.

"He should not be there," she said. "The best thing in the world for a birth is a wise woman. No one wants a man's big dirty hands down there." Sarah Ward smirked, and Maryanne knew she was about to say that *she* wanted a man's big dirty hands down there, but another scream came from below and she did not say it.

"Will you tell us what you were going to tell us, Joan Beattie?" asked Maryanne, and Joan smiled.

"Well—it is that when my little brothers and sisters would die, you know, my mother used to say their spirits were flying to Heaven and their bodies being received into the earth," she said, musingly, to none of them in particular. There are people like this, Maryanne thought, who know when a story is needed. "Or perhaps she would say their bodies were *joining* the earth—I cannot remember the exact word she used," Joan went on. "But I do remember the impression that I formed of this in my young head, and it was a very peaceful imagining, that my brother or my sister would be lying on soft sweet grass, green as green, green as an emerald, and a little white winged thing would come out of their mouths, not a bird, but winged, with bird's wings, feathered, but no beak, no eyes, and swoop off and away into the sky, quick as a flash. And then I imagined that my brother or my sister would begin to sink gently into the grass, and—they were peaceful, you know, asleep, in my mind—that the earth would become soft, just like—you know, as if it were milk pudding, or something like that—and it would pool and my brother or my sister would go gently in and it would close back over them and for a moment there would be a lump which would then sink down and the grass would be just as soft and green and sweet as it had been before. Where I lived there were fields of grass like this. Before I was sent to Liverpool, which is a dirty great place, there were fields, and I imagined all the little children and everybody who had died down there. And although I had seen the coffins go many times into the dirt of the churchyard, I could not picture any person that I loved, or any person at all, in that sad place. Instead I would close my eyes and pretend we had carried that person out onto the grass and laid them down there, not in any box at all, to be—yes—received."

Sarah Ward had been watching her as she spoke. "Why are you here, Joan Beattie?" she asked her. "You are too good for the likes of us." Sarah's face was shining, her cheeks rosy, her eyes clear. Maryanne had never seen her so well. She had a sudden, vivid picture in her mind's eye of Sarah Ward as she ought to be, wearing a low green dress and laughing in a public house, perhaps, by a hot hearth.

Joan began to peacefully say, "Well, my dear ..." but she stopped when Mary Christie put her wry white head up from below decks and showed them all her bloody hands.

"A girl," she said, grinning, and then gave a shout of triumph that made them laugh. "Hearty and hale, and the mother sitting up and eating bread and butter. It is the way, sometimes," Mary Christie the witch went on, never saner, putting a neighbourly elbow on the hatch as she stood there, half below and half above. "They are sometimes sick right until the end, and then the babe comes and all is well." A great exhalation came from all the women together.

Into this air of relief there was a sharp rap; it was the carpenter's hammer against the gate of their pen. The women tensed into one another again. Maryanne remembered the carpenter looking at her as she was taken below, and she felt the cold of the coal hole once again all over her body. But Sarah Ward was holding her hand.

The carpenter had come amongst them with two men carrying a large box very like a coffin, each one bearing a narrow end, so they were separated by the length of it. He led these men directly through the midst of the women, looking openly at their faces and bodies with his nailhead eyes as he did so. The men went slowly, watching one another rather than the women, so that the women in their path were compelled to not only part for them but also duck their bonneted heads for fear of hard corners.

"Don't worry yourselves," the carpenter told them, raising his eyebrows, his mouth twisted. "I have built you your nice little locking box that will hold you when you sin, until you are sorry for it, and your souls are much recovered." Maryanne looked around for the chaplain, whose only real use was preventing men from speaking to them, but he had withdrawn himself, just like the doctor.

Mary Christie waggled her red fingers at the carpenter.

"What name will she give the baby?" called Fernsby, ignoring the men.

"Astraea," said Mary Christie, and the women nodded as if this were only to be expected, although Maryanne was sure she had never heard such a name before.

"Let us hear her surname as well, so that we may know how it sounds," said someone.

"Astraea Pitchfork."

"What!" said Sarah Ward. "What manner of name is Pitchfork?"

"It is her family name," said Mary Christie, arch, now patting herself here and there and finally drawing a yellow-stained handkerchief from the pocket of her apron. She began to wipe her bloody hands. "She says she comes from a long line of Pitchforks." And then, looking directly at Maryanne, she said, "Her milk has not come in."

ix. The baby Astraea Pitchfork was a pleated, wiry little creature, her skin flaking and folded, pasted with blood and white wax, her mouth red, her face formed on rage. Her arms moved in jerks, like a puppet on strings poorly handled by its puppet master, and the limp purple tail of the cord lay on her belly. And yet she fit as naturally into the crook of Maryanne's arm as if she were a part of her very body, as if one had grown from the other, or for her.

Maryanne sat dumbly on an empty bed holding the baby, while Mary Christie undid the girl's bodice and took her hard little breast in crooked fingers and gave it a good and practised squeeze. Hot milk sprayed and the baby nuzzled her face back and forth until she felt the nipple and began to suck. Maryanne felt her whole self pour into that greedy mouth. Relief, relief. The pulling of the thorn, the bursting of the blister. The mother in the next bed watched hungrily.

Mary Christie limped off to get one of the stools Sarah Ward so hated and sat herself between them. There was no trace of her madness about her now, whether it had been feigned or real. She was steady with purpose.

Outside the squares of windows, the sea sucked away the sun, and the milk-white stars leaked into the dark of the sky.

"Have you wet-nursed before?" asked the new mother Pitchfork, her voice hoarse from screaming.

"No," said Maryanne.

"That having of a baby is a dreadful wonder," she said. "I cannot believe you have done it too. You are such a little girl."

"Yes, it is dreadful," said Maryanne.

"But where is your baby?" asked Pitchfork. She was not as young as Maryanne, but not very much older, either. Despite having grown too thin, she was pretty, her face bright and raw after her agony, her eyes large and dark. Someone had plaited her brown hair around her head.

The baby smelt of that thing she could not describe. It was like slipping sighing into warm water. She felt her muscles do the remembering for her.

"My baby is with my mother," she said.

"Boy or girl?"

"Boy."

"Name?"

Maryanne paused. "I did not give him one," she said. "They did not allow it." She paused again. "I hope my mother named him something sensible."

The stars outside the window were cold and perfect, presented like little square pictures of stars in their panes of glass. She could see no moon. The baby sucked and sucked, one breast, and then the other.

"You must keep trying, with the milk," Mary Christie said to the mother. The baby slowed and stopped her sucking and vomited some curds onto Maryanne and then was asleep, her lips still on the nipple. "If you stop, your milk will never come. I will see if I can get you some cream to drink." Then, to Maryanne, she said, "Sleep here in the hospital. We will need you again in the night." But then the hatch above was opened clumsily and the doctor climbed down, the sky against his head, his clothing disheveled and his face red, like a man come home from a hot tavern or a brothel.

"No, you may not sleep here," he said, his voice so loud and deep all three women looked, alarmed, at the sleeping baby in Maryanne's arms, but she did not stir. "Christie, you will fetch Maginn from her berth if she is needed in the night."

As Maryanne slipped out, her breasts light and dry, Lydia Sculthorpe shuffled half asleep into the warm light, her baby still bundled in her arms.

"It is happening again, sir," she said.

Maryanne stood there with the darkness at her back, the night women and their children all laid out in their berths like bodies after a disaster.

"Go to bed," said Mary Christie, looking past Lydia and the doctor at her. So Maryanne closed the door and thus extinguished all light except for a thin golden line below. She dropped to her hands and knees and shuffled forward into the snorts and farts of the sleeping, touching the heavy base of each berth as she passed it, counting until she reached her own.

At night, the hatches were closed and bolted from above, and the barred door was locked and all the women except Elizabeth Duncan whom the captain took were kept inside there. There was air only from the scuttles, which you could not feel at all from the lower berths.

That night was particularly close. She was unspeakably tired. She found her berth and crawled as softly as she could into the space where she lay pressed between Sarah Ward and Maria Green, a woman with a bosom so large it weighted her firmly to the mattress so that she spent the nights complaining that she could not roll over. On the other side of Maria Green lay a bony and sour-smelling woman from London whose name Maryanne had heard but could not remember. The mattress felt damp and her blanket was not there.

Sarah Ward tossed and turned and then abruptly threw her arms around Maryanne, pulled at her, and fell deeply asleep with her sharp cheek pressed into Maryanne's face. Maryanne lay with her nose and mouth pressed into the pillow that smelt of sea and, beneath that, vomit, and beneath that, straw, down below in the place where she did not choose to be. But it was where she was, and she put her own arms around Sarah Ward and went to sleep, until she should be needed. But she was not called upon to wet-nurse again that night.

"Maryanne," whispered Sarah, poking her in the side. Maryanne rose out of sleep and sat up, but Sarah pushed her back down.

"What is wrong?" asked Maryanne.

"Hush! Speak softly! I had a dream about our arrival, and I knew I must wake you," Sarah hissed. "We must have a serious conversation about what we will do when we get there."

"Should not we wait until morning?"

"No—I will forget. We must talk now. I have heard that all the men there will come onboard the ship and we will stand before them and they will choose from amongst us their little serving girls. I will be all right because of my red hair and my good teeth, and I can show an ankle and smile. But you and I must remain together, and you are such a little mouse they might not even see you. So you must be sure to stand beside me when the time comes. And perhaps we can listen to what the man says—the man who chooses me— and we will come up with something for you when he speaks. You can be a nursemaid if he tells me he has children. I wish you spoke a little rougher, a little more like me. He may hate you for sounding the same as him. He will probably want to be above you in every way. I suppose that Fernsby carries it off, doesn't she? But you are not a Fernsby. Anyway, I shall teach you to speak like a harlot, so that if we decide that is what the man wants, you can say your Oh Yes Please Sir in a sly little street voice." Sarah Ward sighed, and said, "So that is that," and then she fell asleep again. Maryanne was left to lie awake, turning this over in her head.

x. Mary Piper did not get up with the others when they were roused by the bell in the morning. The women who shared her berth leant over her and felt her skin.
 "Poor little thing," said one of them, crossing herself.
 "Silly girl," said another, crossing herself also. "Too proud for the doctor."
 "No, it was not pride," said the first.
 "Besides, are we not allowed a little pride?" said Joan Beattie from across the room.
 "Well, I suppose we are allowed it, but we might as well all now mark its consequences," said the second woman who had spoken, and all who could see looked down at the dead body lying there, bunched up under the blanket.
 Maryanne was listening, and she could see Mary Piper, but she had become distracted by her breasts, which were fuller and heavier than they had been before. She glanced at the hospital door, but it remained closed.
 There was the creak and thud of the hatch and a pair of shiny boots brought an officer down with his keys. "What cheer is this?" he said, shaking the key in the lock, bringing the barred door open. "Ah, a girl has died? That is a pity. Well, come up on deck and leave her there. The doctor will be down soon." And he went away again.
 Sarah Ward had been folding their blankets to take above to air, but now she flung them away from her. "He ought to care more than that!" she cried. "It ought to be more than a pity!" Maryanne was shushing her, afraid that the officer would hear, but Sarah Ward shoved her, hard, right in her sore breasts, and she stumbled back. "Fucking god damn them all to hell!" Sarah shouted, and then screamed it again, so loud and high the words themselves became nothing but a distorted shriek, and she punched the bulkhead hard, and again, and again, until her knuckles were bloody.
 "Well, now," said Maria Green, picking up the blankets. "There is no call for that."

———

The ocean was buckling in on itself, blue and grey and white, and the ship bounced them like knucklebones. Maryanne took herself off to sit by the stinking bedding. She felt so sick she might vomit. She was thinking of Sarah Ward, who had gone silent and sullen after her outburst below and had been taken off to prepare breakfast. Amongst the women assigned that task was the one from Cork who hated the two of them.

Joan Beattie was down below too, but in the hospital with the gentle young woman from Suffolk, washing Mary Piper's body, stitching her into her shroud. They said they did not mind it, because they had done it before.

Lydia Sculthorpe and her baby were amongst them once more. Lydia sat with her baby in one arm, her son on her lap, and she was swaying, humming. She stroked and stroked the boy's hair with her free hand.

Maryanne leant against the crate of bedding and closed her eyes. Her breasts were aching, dull and constant. She longed for Sarah Ward who hurt her. No, that was not right. She drew her knees up and leant her forehead on them, breathing in the warm sourness of her own skirt. No, she was not longing for Sarah Ward. She worried about her, certainly, just as she worried for Mary Piper, which confused her, because Mary was beyond worry now. She worried for Astraea Pitchfork, who surely would be needing milk again. She worried for herself. She worried for her son. She put that worry away, or tried to. She had got herself turned about in her head, and she could not remember how to put memories away. Water, water, everywhere, she thought, but she was only layering words over a memory of a peaceful little face and warm tight tiny fingers and a sighing little chest which fluttered clear and vivid below.

She felt a subtle change and raised her head. Fernsby was standing above her.

"Dear," she said, companionably. "Are you quite well?"

"Yes, thank you," said Maryanne.

Fernsby looked down at her, evaluating. "And how did you find the new baby and happy mother last night?"

"Very well," said Maryanne.

"Her milk came," called Lydia Sculthorpe across the deck, unexpectedly. "Just before I went out." And she resumed her swaying and humming.

"Well! I suppose that frees *you* of an obligation," said Fernsby to Maryanne.

"Yes," said Maryanne, and felt tears start in her eyes. I want love, she thought, so ashamed it almost suffocated her. Fernsby stooped to look fully into her face.

"You are a peculiar creature," she said, and straightened once more. "Well, good day," she said, but a desire came upon Maryanne to continue in her company, or anyone's, really.

"What I do not know is why she would give her baby a name like Astraea," she said. "Plain names are better. Otherwise you draw attention."

"Well, perhaps she is superstitious," said Fernsby.

"But where has she got the name from? It is so odd." Fernsby regarded her in naked surprise.

"My dear girl! It is the name of our ship," she said. "How can you be ignorant of that?"

Maryanne could not answer this, could not articulate the guillotine she had let down on anything beyond the protracted moment they had together in their little wooden vessel with sea all around them, with nothing of getting on the ship, or being taken to it, or the place she had been taken from. At least the ship was contained; at least the long arms of terror and despair were tempered by the tedium of it, its dull routine, its boring indignities, its smallness. But Fernsby would not care to know this, and so Maryanne did not even attempt it.

Fernsby said, "It is a good name; I must say, it is the saving grace of this ship. That and the wine sherbet. Astraea was a star goddess," she told Maryanne. "She was the celestial virgin, daughter of Astraeus and Eos. She was a better virgin than the Virgin, who had a poor kind of virginity, never knowing the pleasure of a man, but still not spared the agony of childbirth—and that must be worse, surely, a child tearing through a virgin's little body—and whose son grew to be a kind man who she had to watch all tortured and hammered up on a cross for all to see. Astraea was a true virgin who was allowed to keep her body all to herself, even though she did live amongst men. She was the last of the gods, indeed, to be amongst us, to keep hoping that it was not so bad, because of her innocence, I think—all the others had abandoned us and left us to the corruption and horror of it, but she held out here on Earth for a long time. But then, in the end, even she saw the truth of it, the truth of mankind, and shot off up into the stars. And that is the story of Astraea. I think she became a constellation."

"It is a shame she could not stay a girl," said Maryanne.

"No, dear," Fernsby replied. "She was never a girl. She was always the stars, I think." And she strolled away.

When the call to breakfast came, Maryanne sat on as the women and children lowered themselves down the hatch. She went slowly behind them all, with only the chaplain coming after her, but halfway down the ladder she realised this meant she would have very little choice of seat. As she began to feel anxious about this, her bones ached. She suspected her body could not take much more of these terrible preoccupations. She did not know what she could do, and as she went timidly through the barred door, she looked over at their berth where Sarah Ward had shouted and sworn and punched her knuckles bloody. Her own hands were small and ineffectual.

The woman from Cork who hated her was watching from her seat. She was with six others; the tables held eight. This was a problem. The woman gestured at the empty seat. Maryanne looked around but her vision blurred with tears and she could see nothing with any clarity. And so she went and sat.

"Your friend Ward scalded herself badly," the woman said, nudging Maryanne's shoulder with her own. Her face was set, her grey eyes cool. The other women at the table giggled.

There was something happening in the hospital. Maryanne thought she could hear raised voices, but she kept her head down.

"Well?" said the woman. "Don't you care?"

"Yes, I do care," said Maryanne, and the women laughed again. She wished they would be quiet so she could listen to the hospital.

"Do you care to know how she came to be so hurt?"

"Yes," said Maryanne.

"Nosy little slut. It is not for you to know. But I may show you sometime," she said, and pushed her, hard, so Maryanne had to brace. She tried to stand, but the woman gripped her arm to prevent her.

"There is nowhere," said the woman. "Entirely nowhere you might go."

The memory of her own baby came again to Maryanne, quite distinct from Astraea Pitchfork. He had been so tiny and so light and yet had filled her arms and her whole body and the whole entire world, and a surge went through her and she shrugged off the woman and stood. But as she did so, there was a scream and a great clatter from behind the closed hospital door. The doctor shouted, "Right! Enough!" and Astraea began to cry.

The door was opened from within, and flapped emptily for a moment, but then the doctor shouldered through, dragging Sarah Ward by the ear behind him. Her feet were bare and her bodice undone, but her body was all bandaged up underneath. She was crying, and scratching at him, and stumbling along as he pulled her. Her bonnet was off and her red hair was loose. Maryanne had never seen Sarah's hair like this, entirely unbound, rippling waist-length under the sun from the hatches below.

"What—" said the chaplain, who had been skulking off amongst the berths.

"I will be tried no more!" bellowed the doctor, and raised in his other hand a great pair of shears. There were shrieks from amongst the women. The doctor looked up and around at them and stopped, seeming for a moment to waver, but then he shoved Sarah hard to the deck. She landed heavily with a sob on hands and knees and tried to crawl away, but he caught her by the hair and pulled her back. Maryanne rushed forward, arms out.

"Sarah!" she said.

"Down, Maginn!" he roared at her. She tried to fling herself past the chaplain at Sarah Ward, but he pulled her forcefully against his skinny form. She already knew of the hidden strength of men, but still it surprised her, and she froze in his hands. Sarah Ward looked up at her, and the moment stretched: the helplessness of it, as they saw one another there, Sarah injured on the floor, and Maryanne held fast.

The doctor pulled on a hank of Sarah's hair until her chin was up. Sarah was weeping, saying, "No, no," as if he were threatening to cut off her arms, or her head, instead. He wrapped the hair twice around his forearm, a red shock against his white shirtsleeve, and then cut through it with his shears, close to her head. He dropped that piece and yanked her head back again with another and cut through it, sawing a little, nipping her ear. Long clumps of her hair dropped down all around her, laying themselves softly over her shoulders, her bandaged middle, her lap and hands. "You will mark me, sir, you will mark me as bad," she cried.

"Indeed," he said.

XI.   The carpenter had nailed the box outside their pen; it was against a wooden wall below the platform that held the great wheel. Sarah had gone limp on the sailor who pulled her along through the women. It was not Peter Rowe, and Maryanne wished it had been. The wish was not clearly defined, but perhaps she thought Peter Rowe would be gentler, or that there might be some part of Sarah glad to have his hands on her. Sarah was past crying, her eyes staring, her face streaked, her neck bone white and fine, the lines of her skull like an egg's, but bristled with patches of hair, her ears clotted with blood.

The box was a brutal absurdity. One narrow side of it was hinged and closed with a bar. The sailor drew this open and put Sarah inside. She sagged out, so he pushed her in again and closed and barred the door swiftly against her. There was room only for her to stand, and nothing but a narrow opening close to the top. Maryanne, standing as near as she could, against the rail of their pen, could see the tufted remains of Sarah's hair.

The other women were subdued, but they formed themselves into their customary circles. Maryanne expected the chaplain would tell her to sit down, but he left her alone.

"Sarah," she called, but Sarah did not reply.

"It is a frightful thing," said Joan Beattie softly, coming to her side.

"Oh, Joan!" said Maryanne. "What happened?"

Joan stood close, putting a gentle hand on Maryanne's back. "Well," she said. "You know I was down there with Margaret Wright, tending to poor Mary Piper."

"Yes," said Maryanne.

"Sarah Ward came in with a scald all down her front, from cooking—it was boiling water, I think. And so the doctor took her off behind the screen to butter and bandage her. And that was fine. But then he had her remove her stockings and boots. And so she did. And then she went wild, Maryanne! She went entirely wild, shouting and tearing at the screen and pushing at the doctor himself, and I was trying to quiet her, you know, because the new baby was sleeping there, and Mary Piper's body was there, and the doctor was angry. But she was shouting, accusing him of interfering with her—"

"I did not think he would do that!" said Maryanne. "I thought he found us too disgusting."

"Well, no," said Joan, lowering her voice and leaning even closer. "He had said he was going to do an enema on her. And she took it very ill, telling him he was a filthy devil like all the rest of them." Maryanne did not know what an enema was. "She was betrayed," said Joan. "That is what she said. 'You have betrayed me, you have betrayed me.'"

"How long must she stay in there?"

"All day, they are saying."

The chaplain came, and opened the gate, and went and stooped awkwardly by Sarah's box. He glanced around at the women watching him, and shuffled a little so his back was mostly to them. "Ward," he said into the narrow opening. "Have you repented?"

Sarah made a sound.

The chaplain leant in closer, cocking an ear. "What?" he said, and then furrowed his brow, and swung his head around to look at Maryanne. Then he sighed and left Sarah alone, for his breakfast was ready.

Maryanne stood at the railing, trying to think of something to say. Sarah had wanted a story back in the hospital, all those days ago, but Maryanne had disappointed her in that. She let herself remember her mother talking to her as she lay in bed, telling her how to make lace. That, too, would disappoint Sarah, she thought.

"I don't know what to say to you," she said.

There was silence. The ship dipped and bucked, and a man shouted something from above. But then Sarah said, "Maryanne." It was soft but clear, and relief washed through Maryanne so strong she had to take hold of the railing. But then she knew she had to say the right thing in response, or Sarah would fall silent once more.

"That is not my name," she said.

There was another silence, and then Sarah said, "What?"

"Maryanne is not my name," she repeated. "The gaol clerk wrote it down, but it is not what I told him."

"Why?"

"He thought my real name was too absurd."

"What? So he chose you another?" Her voice was rough from crying, but she cleared her throat and added, "Well, what is your name, then?"

"Marie-Antoinette," said the girl with the silly French name, and Sarah

Ward laughed, once, with such loose surprise that the girl could only smile.

"That is ridiculous!" Sarah said, her voice weak but growing clearer as she spoke. "Why the fuck would your mother name you that? Didn't Marie-Antoinette wear silly wigs and get her head chopped off?"

"Yes," said the girl Marie-Antoinette, called Maryanne. "Yes, she got her head chopped clean off her body for wearing silly wigs and being a very stupid queen."

"Oh, my word, girl," said Sarah from her box. "I did not know there was anything in this world left to surprise me." She was silent again, and then she said, "O God, release me! Send me truly mad!" Maryanne glanced at the sky.

"It is nearly the middle of the day," she said. "You are halfway there."

"Will you stay near me?"

"Yes, I will." The girl turned and looked back over the women and girls and their children, all those faces hidden beneath bonnets, anchoring themselves together there in the gaol that kept them from drowning. She sat down with her back against the railing, folding her hands in her lap. Fernsby was pacing the length of their pen, elegant as a doe. Joan Beattie and Elizabeth Duncan were sitting close, their heads bowed together. Mary Christie was holding court over a number of women, and Maryanne could tell from the way she moved her hands she was telling the story of the birth of the baby Astraea. She made some point, raising her hands before her, and the women laughed.

"Are you there?" asked Sarah.

"Yes, I am here."

The woman from Cork looked over, annoyed, from amongst her own companions. And then all sound ended, not only laughter, but all their words and breathing and the sounds of the men and the ship beyond and below.

Lydia Sculthorpe, who had been drowsing, was now awake, her face glazed in horror. As Maryanne watched, she saw Lydia and the baby in her arms slowly become suspended in the air. The ship and all the women dissolved, and Maryanne felt herself dissolve, and for a blink Lydia and her baby were simply there floating alone above the unmoving ocean, their shadow falling small across the waves. A little white winged thing soared from them.

"Oh dear," said Joan Beattie, rising, and the world came back. "So it has finally happened. Oh, that is most terribly cruel."

"What?" said Elizabeth Duncan.

Mary Christie creaked up and over to Lydia. She unwrapped the limp baby and then wrapped her back up again, but this time covering the face as well, which was as little and as blue as a duck's egg. Lydia's friends moved around her and they all became perfectly still, leaning in to her, like a flower half closed.

The sun sank from its apex and the shadows stretched beneath them. The grey sea sighed low. As the last of the sun rippled over the waves it brought a swell of gentle colour. The girl stood, and looked out, and saw nothing but a sweet green field going as far as the eye could see.

Kate Shepherd, *Eavesdropper*

Kate Shepherd, *Earth*

A PUBLIC BENCH

SUZANNE BUFFAM

In loving memory of John Scott Stephen (1920-1996) and Audrey Blanche Stephen (1925-2009) reads a small black plaque in need of new paint on the backrest. If this bench belongs to anyone, then, surely it belongs to the Stephens. But it's truer to say that they are renting it, or rather their descendants are, for as long as they care or can afford to from the city, which retains at public expense several year-round employees to combat the pigeons, vandals, sea-spray, and winter storms, and which likewise maintains memorial picnic tables, memorial flower planters, and memorial drinking fountains at ever-diminishing intervals along this scenic coastal shore, settled as it was by the British in the nineteenth century after several thousand years of continuous habitation by the Coast Salish people of the Songhees First Nation, who faced their homes into the wind and laid their dead away in trees between the tideline and the meadows the better to enjoy the bounty of the landscape and the nearby Salish Sea, following in turn the Paleolithic footsteps that trailed the bison, the caribou, the musk oxen, the horses, and the woolly mammoths across the Bering land bridge from Siberia. Still, while I'm sitting here sipping my tea on it, watching the boats and beyond the boats the ships go by, breathing in the brackish sweet funk of ocean air which may as well be the breath of time itself, I can't help feeling that this bench belongs, however fleetingly, to me. Or else that I belong to it.

WOMAN RUNNING

SUZANNE BUFFAM

Look at that strange woman running. There is no bus in sight. No one seems to be chasing her. No one else is even on the street at this hour. She is not running very quickly, mind you, but she is definitely not walking. She cannot possibly be jogging in that sarong. Maybe she is simply running late. If so, for what? Even the songbirds and the sirens are asleep. If only we could get a better look at her face. But she has crossed the street now, she has passed the bus stop, and she has not slowed down. In fact she seems to be picking up speed. All we can see now are the ghostly soles of her sandals lifting from the pavement as she sprints into the mist. How long has she been running? How much longer is she going to be running?

TREE ROOTS
KIRSTEN KASCHOCK

No. He studies a single blade of grass.

This is how my own mind lies, low, looking
for men who expend their low lives lost
in looking. Do not think me circular. I'm no
dog spiraling into nest. Plus, I cannot by any means
sleep. Color is to blame. It will not be arrested.
Me, I shall die. There is only the matter of manner.
Ends require discrete methodologies, forms breed
functions no scientist predicts. No man—none
—can claim honestly to be *of science*. He does
not know. But I do. It is a weight I carry
in my palette. Therefore, I am no man and this
exile is both relief and a keening. Imagine a rung
bell: it grieves *because* it is hollow. One is given only
to sound one's lack. If you climb the ladder of joy
toward a still life—think what cut stem means
to she who interrogated the flower, who scratched
up winter wood for the kiln. There is no art
for her, no bee she should catch in the melody
of her hair. Stung her whole body over, she is
able as *a bell*. Thus, the swelling. Children pour
out: crows from emptied field, having eaten, having
assumed. Green is not for long. Blue is a portal.
A blade of grass fails wielding. And yellow? It
varies as the light does: blinding or
revelatory, it is the stain of God.

THE CRISIS OF IMAGINATION (CATULLUS 26)
MIKE LALA

The underlying cobblestones point us to another age
of thieves, the second homes, the winds that bluster, still, in vain.

Even now, the forest air smells of pine, then ash like chimes,
mocking time entombed in perfect sunlight, as we,

fugitives of smog and mindless hunger, rabid as our debt,
open windows, coming home, twisting closed the shades.

OLD MASTERS
GRAHAM FOUST

Some people want to put a fist
through a Vermeer, and some don't,
and you're not the only one who thinks
that you're the only one who's both.

Scenes in air like prosody—white
on an apple, light near a pear,
as paint sets up a plane that words can seize.

That's still life, loose memory,
your head into death,
the disintegrating tape
of following up.

CIVIL DISCOURSE
GRAHAM FOUST

Or better yet, to've been
thrown weirdly clear of it,
a few masks to the wind,
a sky-giant bell, the middle past
passed up for one more star.

Scratch that and scratch
that and scratch that and
scratch that—a hyphen in
the word for what
the knife's been in thus far.

ESSAY

EYE AND MIND
CALVIN GIMPELEVICH

At twenty-three, I learned I am resistant to oxycodone. The discovery came two hours after surgery, as anesthesia wore off and I found myself on the couch of a shared house, suddenly excruciatingly conscious. The resistance is not only to oxycodone, but alcohol and painkillers in general. My liver is hyperefficient at breaking them down. I had aspirin, a worthless prescription, and all the brutal sensations of a torso cut and resewn.

    A friend of a friend, a weed grower, came with indica paste and the promise that it would have no psychotropic effects, only physical dulling. I disliked and avoided marijuana for the anxious internality it spawned but thought the circumstances demanded trying. Nothing happened.

Hours later, I was in bed with my then-girlfriend, trying to sleep, when a series of grotesque bulbous dripping cartoonish figures marched behind my eyelids to a warped folkish tune. The woman beside me transformed into an elongated peach dinosaur, eyes flat on top of her head like an alligator's. Time stopped and my first coherent thought was that I had lied: my thoughts contained images after all.

Aphantasia comes from the Greek *phantasía* (imagination), its "a" conferring a lack. The most frequent poetic description of aphants is people for whom the mind's eye is blind. My thoughts are like an audiobook: mostly coherent, transcribable. I understand the concept of something like an apple verbally, without image. It's like reading a dictionary.

The lack relates only to images one wants to conjure. Involuntary imagery, in hallucinations, dreams, and something neuroscientists call "flashes" remain. The Greek seems misleading. I don't lack an imagination in any conventional sense of the term—if anything, have an overactive imagination, prone to fantasies with grand narrative arcs—but "imagination" has its own root. The ability to form new and creative ideas is so bound up with visualization in the English language that the very concept of an imagination is drawn from the Latin term for picture.

I remember sitting in a garden in California in the early spring, when I was twenty years old, sunlight forming a halo behind my girlfriend, dark hair tinted golden in flyaway strands, surrounded by deer paths and flowers; the tender shoots of new greens. I remember shielding my eyes, barely able to look at her for the brightness enclosing her, thinking I should appreciate this moment, not because it was special but because it matched the cinematic aesthetic for an absent idealized time.

Even though this is a visual memory, in that it is a memory of an image, I experience it as a set verbal descriptors.

At this point, in my thirties, I have consumed hundreds of movies, millions of pictures, and probably thousands of books. They are filters through which I view and narrate my life, the way others use biblical tales. Instead of detecting

God's hand in my experiences and trials, I look at a woman seated at a picnic table in a sunny garden and see a style of memory sequence in films.

Not just any sequence. The sunlit garden relates to the memories of a widower; the happiness preceding the tragedy forming the backstory for a hero or villain. The films my girlfriend reminded me of weren't subtle—and I found myself projecting the emotions of those stories onto myself; feeling nostalgic for the present (in that unremarkable moment), as if it represented the now unattainable joys of my past. I remember wondering if that afternoon would haunt me, if it would come to symbolize youth, ease, and pleasure. And, because of these thoughts, in a strange way, it has.

How many more deserving things have I forgotten, while the image of sun and woman remains?

Two of my friends were moving and I was helping, with another friend, on a long rainy day, hauling their many objects in a small flat-bedded truck. We were hungry. The pizza was late. First a problem with the order, then a problem receiving calls in the new apartment, not realizing the delivery had come and gone away. I started describing food—something I am very good at—to the annoyance of my friends. Thick-crusted pizza with red sauce and glistening weighted cheese holding crisped mushrooms and slivers of pepper. Ramen in a cloudy miso broth, dropping in a soft-boiled egg, pushing a chopstick through its tender white so orange yolk opens and spills over noodles. Salty things. Spicy things. Sweets. Chocolate-hazelnut spread on bread and butter.

I only learned recently that many aphants are unable to conjure sense memories. Which is not to say I learned of a new absence in myself, but that other people relive the smell and taste and textures of meals, as if meals reconstituted themselves to be eaten again, which seems distracting, but explains why other people experience food cravings and I do not. How painful, that descriptive game. How close and strange to have ghosts invading your palate, for digested flavors to revive themselves, stimulating physical want.

Capacity varies across the condition. For instance, I have auditory memories where some aphants do not. Songs get stuck in my head. I can imagine sounds and conversation and "hear" words as I write them. It is as difficult for me to conceptualize life without these private acoustics as it is for others to grasp my blank projector.

I have many descriptions, filed, like the one in that garden. If I don't, it seems my life will vanish, that I won't have any record of experience to hold on to, so I carry notebooks and describe the mist hanging over a field in winter, trying to set that vision into something at least as permanent as I am. I want to correct the absence, honing narratives around pictures in a way I don't bother to with those things that come easily, auditory impressions, or tactile sensations I have accepted as ephemeral. There is something consumptive about it, the encasing and preservation of memories, like insects in resin, with words. Sometimes it seems that I could have just as easily been a photographer.

Think of the tourists who take pictures of monuments with the same angles and framing as the (better) photos in the gift store. Does the professional image expand appreciation—or stifle perspectives of one's own?

I saw the New York City skyline, as interpreted by a theme hotel in Las Vegas, before the thing in itself, and its likeness in a thousand cartoons, photos, and movies, before visiting either of them. I remember the illusive feeling, born of visual familiarity, on my first trip, that I had already digested Manhattan—surely, subtly, privileging those impressions that matched my preconception.

Sometimes I try to manipulate life (for myself, and others) by culling unflattering photos. The survivors tell of a happy poignant life of good haircuts and clear skin. Because I did photographic modeling as a young adult and have maintained friendships with photographers into the present, some of these are quite good. Even though I remember my mental states in these pictures, know that they are cherry-picked from a series of less successful photos, and am aware that the pictures are digitally altered, I find myself jealous. Look at how attractive, how happy I was then. Why does the present feel so mundane when I have this proof of extraordinary, symbolic living touched then?

Baudrillard says, "The obsession with becoming slimmer and slimmer is an obsession with becoming an image, and therefore transparent, an obsession with the disembodied ideality which is that of film stars. Disembodiment is the price paid for immortality, extreme slimness being the only way to pass through death."

Replace *slimness* with *polish*. The obsession with looking polished; seeing oneself as a film or photograph from above. Mimicking images that are larger than life, and so outside it. Something flat, immortal, and enviable. *Possessing* as opposed to *being in*.

I went to *The New York Earth Room* in Manhattan, mainly for the charm of knowing that a loft, otherwise fully capable of housing lucrative business or people, had been filled with dirt since 1977. I (thought) I knew what to expect: 250 cubic yards of dark earth in an empty, white-walled apartment, viewable from a single angle, with knee-high plexiglass separating visitors from the twenty-two inches of dirt. I knew that the same caretaker had raked, watered, and scrubbed mold from the installation for decades, and that I could see it for free.

Its lobby provided the same sudden respite from noise and cold as any building. I don't remember if I took an elevator or the stairs. A buzzer, listing the art piece's full name, was pressed at some point to get in. A smaller lobby, specific to the installation, held the caretaker, flyers, and desk. It looked like the entry to any gallery with white walls and wood flooring, except for the sudden termination of that floor beneath what seemed like a freshly plowed field. Bare bulbs shone from the white ceiling; a few simple rectangular windows brought light from outside. The air was warm and loamy, palpable in a way the atmosphere of interior space normally is not. Instead of being neutrally climate controlled and antiseptic, the air seemed full of that dirt holding still. Most of the loft was empty, but the absence seemed weighted and tangible. Emptiness became its own kind of presence and I became so engaged with this heightened awareness of space that I forgot to regulate my breathing, until the woman beside me startled, and I realized she could hear me.

This awareness followed me outside the exhibition, a realization of negative space, that fundamentally changed my perception of life. Before visiting this installation, I'd had no awareness of architecture beyond that required for physical navigation: the unconscious discernment of apertures and blockages in the form of doorways and walls. I moved through the world in an almost wholly interior space. *The New York Earth Room* made me aware that my life in cities has, in some ways, been a life within others' intents and visions—and also that, instead of being eternal, inert, or given to me by an abstracted deistic other, such environments could be impacted by my own advocacy and vision.

Photographs of the *Earth Room* were forbidden by the artist, Walter De Maria, and none of the pictures I've seen evoke the experience of seeing it in person—but, in a way, a still from Andrei Tarkovsky's *Stalker*, showing three men wandering through a dreamscape of sand dunes between abandoned concrete pillars, lit from above, in a space much larger and more imposing than De Maria's loft, does. The movie comes even closer, with sounds of droplets, echoes, and footsteps, as the camera tracks difficult physical motion and sand puffs out in white clouds.

Elaine Scarry: "At the moment we see something beautiful, we undergo a radical decentering. Beauty, according to Weil, requires us 'to give up our imaginary position as the center. . . . A transformation then takes place at the very roots of our sensibility, in our immediate reception of sense impressions and psychological impressions.' . . . we find we are standing in a different relationship to the world than we were a moment before. It is not that we cease to stand at the center of the world, for we never stood there. It is that we cease to stand even at the center of our own world. We willingly cede our ground to the thing that stands before us."

Certain images and experiences remove me from my center. Not all of them are beautiful, but because there is something beautiful about the fact of decentering, because beauty might be indistinguishable from presence, they are cast in a beautiful haze.

Which complicates the quasi-idyllic memory of a woman in a garden in spring. If you stripped the cinematic halo, I would not have been conscious of the moment, and it would be long forgotten by now. But, because of the halo and its relationship to movies, I became the audience of my own life, hovering above the situation, consuming and scrutinizing signals for how I *should* feel, instead of experiencing what I actually did. But then, in another step, because in films the halo signals beauty, I looked closer at it, taking in, with a mild decentering, what I probably would have ignored. Cinema provides a language for noticing *(being in)* while simultaneously encouraging me to view myself as an image *(possessing)*.

Is there a difference between the garden where, because I think a moment *should* be beautiful or meaningful it is, and the *Earth Room*, where the sensation came by surprise, on its own?

I used to sit in cold rooms, surrounded by space heaters, naked, immobile for twenty or thirty minutes, observed by groups of a dozen or more.

This happened in near ecclesiastical silence, to the scratching of charcoal, pencils, and sometimes audible breath. An aura of silence pervaded despite the music—even dance music—often playing in the background. This silence came from the effort of looking; of pulling art from the raw materials of perception and skill.

I stood or sat or contorted myself on a platform draped in fabric that may or may not have a chair. Poses ranged from gestures—crouching, twisting stretching—that lasted a minute to classic static positions that went for six weeks. It is an almost perfect job for a writer: paid to hold still and think. Despite boredom, cramping, and pain, it provides a sense of leisure, to sit while the artists struggle.

I had some of the best and most pleasant senses of my body on those platforms. This had nothing to do with exhibitionism or my appearance, but the knowledge that my actual body, the atoms, follicles, and personality forming myself, constituted the perfection these artists had to get down. The closer they came to the reality of my being, the closer they came to success. The perfection I represented did not require my specific body, except as a manifestation of reality in that moment; I could have easily been (and often was) replaced by a different object or person: another model, an object, fruit bowls.

We have the tendency toward symbolic shorthand, to make caricatures, to look at a model and draw a mix of expectations and memories. Hands are rounder and bonier than expected, skulls larger, eyes lower in the head. The artists struggled. Instructors wandered with helpful comments, the most frequent being Draw what you see, not what you think that you see. Basic lessons, but even experienced drawers put their own noses on other faces, draw generic ears instead of a model's unique protrusions.

You could say that first, instead of painting or drawing, students are learning to see, then to make their hands obey what they see. The model ceases to be a cohesive figure, becomes a complicated series of lights and shapes and shadows, then joins into a person again. Both perspectives are necessary—plus difficult intangible things: the sense of motion, expression, personality. They were asked to experience the world directly, to rely on their own perception instead of the picture that lay in their heads, to take things as they are instead of as anything else. If they are successful, the artwork becomes an event in itself.

How tempted I am to buy gift shop reproductions of beautiful artworks, as if they could re-create not only the reality of that piece, but a moment in time. What I want is not the likeness of a Picasso, Martin, LeWitt, but the emotional reality of seeing them and being decentered, a feeling I would like undiminished, on tap, at all times. The idea that an image can be possessed—which, in the case of a painting, it can be, but the intangible attached, what the image represents is already dispersing through time. The irony that even thinking about pausing, possessing, preserving is the beginning of recentering and loss. The inability to stop time.

I've learned that recording a memory saps its vitality, giving it fully to the paper, so only the recording exists, as opposed to the looser, richer, more changeable version floating in my psyche, which makes me reticent to write certain things, or to wait until the memory is fading, committing it to external storage. There is a flash of extra engagement while writing it down—as there was recording the woman, the halo, the garden—before ceasing to be part of my internality; gift shop facsimiles of my own life.

A consolation for lack of mental image is my capacity for sober hallucination. Such happenings are infrequent and usually pleasant. The first two happened in second grade, in love with a book, C. S. Lewis's Christian symbolic fantasia, *The Lion, the Witch and the Wardrobe*, for the first time. I was daydreaming in the car and looked up and the sky was black with some bird described in the novel, completely overrun by the flock in a way that does not happen in contemporary San Francisco, thudding with the majestic heft of their wings.

Later, at school, my teacher turned into a faun. For a few moments, outside the auditorium, I saw him shirtless and goat legged, balancing on cloven hooves, garlanded with leaves and flowers as his human mouth continued giving teacherly instructions beneath horns and pointed ears. Apparently Lewis had a similar image: the entire Narnia series came from a picture of a faun clutching an umbrella and parcels in a snowy wood that popped into his head.

There are maybe a dozen others: the abandoned CD player that looked, to me, like the eye of a huge monster simmering, like a crocodile in water, mostly under the ground; the image of a space twink that came during acupuncture: a slim naked erect young man outlined in white with an ecstatic sense about him, in outer space, whose transparent body showed cosmos and stars. None of these temporary visions lasts long. In another trick of atypical neural firing, they are etched more clearly than other pictures. It feels like I could almost conjure the space twink's image, that if I tried just a little bit harder, I could see my teacher, the faun. There are so many things that it feels like I should be able to record, that I want to preserve, but the moment of trying is also the moment of knowing they're gone. Looking too closely at anything makes it dissolve.

FICTION

SUBOPTIMAL
MEGAN CUMMINS

Emma walked the length of the waiting room, looking at her phone. There was a new message from him, a dose of attention that thrilled her into feeling good. They were at the beginning of something, and she thought about that something, their beginning, as though she were already looking back on it. This was how they had met, at the right time for both of them.

She sat nearest the door from which she would be called. Tridents of cold sunlight struck the windows, everything made brighter by the glimmer coming off the East River. A nurse called her name, and Emma followed her into an exam room, stepped on the scale, and declined the offer for the figure to be converted from kilograms to pounds. She confirmed she wasn't dizzy even though her blood pressure was low.

"Good to see you, Emma." Dr. Castillo stuck his head into the room. "Come into my office."

At each visit, first thing, Emma scanned the degrees from Yale and Johns Hopkins on the wall and tried once more to get an accurate count of the number of small table clocks Dr Castillo had on display without making it obvious she was counting. They covered his desk and bookshelves, were pushed behind his computer, and peered down from on top of his cabinets. Some amount of neck-craning was involved to see them all. Last time she'd counted seventy-one.

She didn't see that someone else stood in the room, quietly posted in the corner. He looked Emma up and down quickly and a decision passed over his face.

"Did you hear me? Is that okay?" Dr. Castillo asked.

Emma found that Dr. Castillo spoke so much and so quickly about things she didn't have the training to understand that sometimes her attention lapsed.

"I'm sorry, what?"

"With your permission I'd like my new fellow to sit in on the appointment—Dr. Chen. As you know, Yorkville is a teaching hospital. And you're an interesting case that I think Fred could learn from."

Her fingers twitched quickly against her cheeks, where a malar rash had bloomed. Emma looked at Fred, waiting for him to say something. When he didn't, she sat down, putting her bag and coat on the empty chair next to hers. "You've said that before. I'm interesting. Sure, I don't mind."

Dr. Castillo clicked through Emma's chart. "Female, thirty-six years old, diagnosed systemic lupus at twenty-four, prior to that had two DVTs, she has Raynaud's, secondary Sjögren's, is triple positive for antiphospholipid antibody syndrome, had been stable and seeing me since 2017 when diagnostics indicated lupus nephritis last year. Which as you know it's unusual for kidney involvement to present for the first time so long after diagnosis, but it happens. I wanted to do a kidney biopsy last year but opted not to when the protein in the urine melted away with prednisone, but now DNA is high again and complements are low and protein is back so we're here to figure out what to do so we can hopefully avoid long-term kidney disease."

Dr. Castillo looked at Emma. "Did I miss anything?"

"I think that covers it."

"I told you," Dr. Castillo turned his head slightly, speaking out of the corner of his mouth to Fred. "She was already in two of my research studies, and now that she has kidney involvement, she's the only patient I have who's in all three."

"It's like I've evolved into the patient that fits all your needs," Emma said. "People pleasing to a new level."

Dr. Chen decided not to laugh. Dr. Castillo didn't react; he only listened to patients after he'd asked a question.

"Okay, Dr. Chen is caught up," Dr. Castillo said. "Emma, how are you feeling?"

"Tired," she said. "A lot of joint pain. Frequent urination. Some shortness of breath."

Dr. Castillo pelted Emma with his usual barrage of questions, the same ones every time: Headaches? Stomach pain? Swollen feet? Swollen glands? Open sores on her fingers? Diarrhea? Bleeding? Rash? Fever?

"When was the last time you had to take your Valtrex?"

Fred's attention darted toward Emma. She recoiled from it.

"Last week," she said, looking at her hands.

"Here's what we'll do," Dr. Castillo said. "We'll schedule you for a kidney biopsy before the holidays. In the meantime, instead of prednisone, I'm going to give you a pulse steroid treatment of dexamethasone, but we need to figure out your dose. What's 2.5 times 62?"

Dr. Castillo looked at Emma, who looked back, horrified. Of all the things he'd asked, this was the worst.

Dr. Chen said his first words, spoken softly. "It's mean to ask patients to do math."

It wasn't what Emma had expected him to say, but at least he'd said something.

The elevator doors opened at ground level, and Emma paused in the lobby just short of the automatic doors.

She hadn't worn makeup, had come unbathed and in yoga pants. The anxiety she'd stowed away during the appointment came out as a laugh. Her ungloved hands were already draining of color as she typed into her phone.

Given all that do you still want to meet for our date on Friday?

Emma's messages were friendly but tentative. She gestured toward making light of what had happened. Fred, though, was shaken, furious with himself for freezing in the exam room, and he replied only to plan the logistics of their date—no emojis, no *can't wait to see you*s. Emma seemed stubbornly against suggesting anything, and so Fred asked her to meet him early in the evening at a basement bar in Williamsburg, a location that was convenient for neither of them.

Fred arrived early and when he sat down the waitress was still delivering candles to each table. Five minutes passed and he watched the maraschino cherry stain his whiskey sour red. He tried again to unravel the past few weeks. He'd met Emma during his first deep breaths after the precarious time on the waitlist for the fellowship. He liked the sound of their voices together, talking, and their texts and phone calls had been important to him, a part of his day he made sure not to neglect. This was life happening, he'd thought—his career, her. He'd faltered in Dr. Castillo's office. She wasn't easy anymore.

A thick set of red velvet curtains covered the entrance. Fred watched them rustle, and Emma appeared, momentarily tangled in the fabric before she stepped all the way in, looking around. She walked toward him, clutching a pair of black leather gloves in hands that were so ice-white he wondered if she'd even worn them. Then he remembered her Raynaud's, and her medical chart opened in his mind, all he saw as she stood over him.

"Is it strange to say nice to meet you, since we already met?" She smiled, draping her long camel coat over the back of her chair.

Fred rose and kissed her cheek, finding it was awkward to touch, but also awkward not to. They'd already had sex on Facetime. They'd both admitted never to have done that before meeting in person—and touching Emma in person was something Fred had thought about, waited for, a pleasure overwhelmed by Dr. Castillo's rapid-fire rundown of all her ailments.

A glass of water had been waiting for her at the table, and she dipped the tips of all ten of her fingers into it and smoothed her hands through her staticky hair. Fred watched, bewildered.

"I was glad you still wanted to meet." She grabbed the ear of an empty chair at their table and squeezed it. "I mean, I still wanted to see you. So, I'm glad you wanted to see me, too."

He didn't know where to begin.

"I told you I was a fellow at Yorkville," he said after a moment. "Why didn't you tell me you were Dr. Castillo's patient?"

"I didn't know you were in rheumatology." She was chewing on her chapped lips now; a flake of red lipstick caught on her tooth. "You just said internal medicine."

"But Yorkville was something we had in common."

"I'm sure there are many women on Tinder who have been to Yorkville," she said.

Fred didn't have another point to make. He'd lost the excitement he'd felt in not knowing her yet. Instead, he felt he knew too much. She took a tube of Burt's Bees from her bag and ran it over her lipstick, staining the bulb of the lip balm red.

"I know it's not typical to talk medical history before the first date, but I hope you were planning at some point to tell me you have herpes?" He tried to say it with a laugh, but he found he couldn't.

She looked from side to side, eyes wide. To her wine glass she said, "Look, I don't know why you're being mean. I take Valtrex for cold sores. Honestly, it's a miracle drug, and it changed my life. I'm not ashamed."

"The way I found out was just strange," Fred said helplessly.

"What if it was for genital herpes?" Her eyes grew stormy with an argument, trapping him as she spoke. "Would you judge a patient for that?"

"You're not my patient."

"You're only empathetic at work?"

"Maybe we should talk about something else," he said.

"Maybe." Her voice was lower; the verve had slipped out of her.

"Maybe one day we'll laugh about it," Fred said.

"Maybe," she said again, fishing in her bag for her phone that had begun to ring. She turned the screen toward him.

"It's your boss," she said. "Hello? Hi, Dr. Castillo."

Fred stayed very still and quiet.

"Okay. I understand. Are you sure your fellow is okay with coming in on a Sunday? All right, I'll be there." She ended the call. "He wants to do a skin biopsy before the kidney biopsy. For research."

"It's a good idea," Fred said, his interest piqued. "If we get enough data that shows a skin biopsy can tell us the same thing as a kidney biopsy, we wouldn't have to rely on such an invasive procedure."

"I know. He told me."

"And since you've already started steroids, it's better to do it as soon as possible, before the drugs really kick in."

"I know," she said again. "That doesn't mean you have to say yes to coming in on a Sunday."

"It's my job." Fred shrugged, draining his drink. "I do have to say yes."

A grim look settled on Emma's face. The waitress asked if they needed anything else, and at their silence set the bill between them. Fred took it, waving Emma's outstretched card away.

"I'm sorry if this was strange," he said. "I wanted to see you in person, to apologize—I should have said something in Dr. Castillo's office. That's on me for not."

"Neither of us said anything," Emma said. "We can't be blamed for the shock."

"I suppose we shouldn't talk or see each other anymore."

Emma patted her pockets for her gloves, and she pulled them out along with a bent metro card. "You'll see me Sunday," she said.

Emma rode the train home alone. Right up until she pulled back the red velvet curtain, she'd expected to laugh with him. Instead she'd felt cornered, exposed as an optimist, and a fool. Despite her pronouncement in the bar that she wasn't ashamed, she grew ashamed as she sat on the train. Then she willed the shame into steel. Fred was right. Nothing was her fault.

Why hadn't he said something? Maybe he was terrified. Or maybe it was the opposite. Maybe he loved his boss. She didn't know him that well.

Her illness had gotten in the way of her relationships before—she couldn't be relied upon to act in a way people thought a woman her age should—but never this obviously. He'd been kind, curious. He'd listened. He'd laughed. And she'd really liked him.

Empty and locked on Sundays, half of the lights off, the medical center had an apocalyptic feel. Emma crossed the street without looking for traffic and Fred flattened his arm against the door to hold it open from the inside.

She slipped past him.

"Thanks for coming in," he said.

"Whatever you want from me, you can have."

Everything she said seemed to mean something else.

They walked side by side to the elevator, silent as they went upstairs. In the small exam room attached to Dr. Castillo's office, Fred asked if she wanted to change into a gown. She shook her head and removed her coat and then the oversize knit cardigan she was wearing. Underneath was a thin black tank top. He already knew her breasts were small, and he turned away. She became aware he wanted to look at her; he felt almost sick because of it.

"Dr. Castillo will be here soon," he said. "But just so you know, this is a punch biopsy. I'll give you a shot of lidocaine to numb the area, and then the punch will take tissue about the size of a pencil eraser. You'll have a scar, but it will fade over time."

"A scar?" she said.

"You don't have to go through with it."

She shrugged. "Something to remember you by."

Dr. Castillo appeared in the door, talking fast as usual over the squeal of hand sanitizer squirting from the wall dispenser. He pulled his hand away too quickly and the foamy solution splashed on the floor.

"I'm supervising Dr. Chen today," Dr. Castillo said. "He probably told you you'll feel some pressure, but it shouldn't hurt too much."

Dr. Castillo rounded the exam table to stand by Fred, who froze for a moment. He placed a hand on Emma's arm; her eyes were fixed on his fingers and the cold swipe of an alcohol wipe over her skin. He drained the lidocaine into her arm and in the small white bubble that appeared he aimed the punch and twisted.

"A little deeper," Dr. Castillo said.

Emma felt pressure, corkscrewed pain. They were wrong; it did hurt. Her eyes flickered to the computer in the corner, which had timed out and gone dark. Fred pulled the chunk of skin free from her arm. He blotted the glistening film of blood and made a tidy stitch, closing the hole in her he'd just made. Emma shivered.

"Beautiful," Dr. Castillo said as Fred stuck a label on the sample. "When did interventional radiology schedule you for the biopsy?"

"The Tuesday before Christmas," Emma said.

"We'll talk after. Merry Christmas."

Dr. Castillo slapped the door frame twice on his way out, leaving Fred to hand Emma a clipboard of forms. He explained the first, a questionnaire to assess the mental health of lupus patients before and after a kidney biopsy. She answered the questions quickly, barely pausing to read each one.

"And what's this?" Her eyes scanned the consent form that followed.

"If you agree, we'd also like to take an additional sample of your kidney for research."

"More of my kidney? How much more?"

"Not much. The radiologist would never take more than a total very small amount."

She looked over the form.

"I'm sorry," Fred said. "I thought Dr. Castillo had talked to you about this."

She trailed her pen down the paper, paused at the signature line. Then she signed swiftly, dated in large looping figures.

"Whatever you want from me," she said.

"You'll feel pressure but not pain," the radiologist said, the second time Emma had heard this.

She lay on her stomach and the fentanyl nudged her brain into a half-sleep. The room was dimly lit so the doctor—she'd forgotten his name already—could see the monitor and guide the needle beneath her skin. She was so relaxed she almost wished the biopsy wouldn't end, as though she were getting a massage, but soon they were wheeling her to a recovery bay, still flat on her stomach on the stretcher.

Fred was standing outside the curtain.

He said something to the nurse, who left Emma with him.

"You can probably roll over now," he said.

She pushed herself up on her fists, winced as she rolled over her hip. Fred pushed the button to raise the back of her bed.

"That's good," she said. "You don't have any reason to be in this part of the hospital."

"You don't know that."

The fentanyl was wearing off, leaving a headache in its place. Emma had hardly slept the night before, hadn't eaten anything since yesterday on doctor's orders, and had felt heartbroken since she'd last seen Fred. It wasn't really love, she knew, but he'd given up on her, and calling it love felt like revenge.

She looked beyond the open curtain. Some of the nurses and doctors had dressed up for the holidays, reindeer headbands and snowflake earrings. A flashing strand of lights tangled up in a stethoscope. Daily her kidneys accumulated damage; her clothes didn't fit because the steroids made her eat day and night, and she'd found a man she liked only to watch him handed her medical records and recoil at the sight of who she was on the inside.

He was standing beside her bed, and she wondered if she could make him, if not in love with her, then a little bit obsessed with her, even if obsession was an emotion in foreclosure.

"It was nice of you to stop by," she said. "A little weird, though."

"Is someone in the waiting room for you?" he asked. "I can go get them."

"I'm here alone."

"They won't release you without someone to take you home." Fred looked toward the exit.

"My reluctant neighbor is coming. In exchange, I'm dogsitting while she's out of town."

"I'll take you home," he said quietly. "If it's not too late to tell your neighbor not to come."

The nurse returned to check if Emma was bleeding. He looked Fred up and down. Fred's fingertips were on her sheets, near her body, and he curled them quickly into a fist.

Emma pulled her blanket up to her chest when the nurse had gone. Now he wanted to take her home. Hadn't he taken enough from her? And why did she want to see just how much he could take?

"You can take me home," she said finally, "but it doesn't get me off the hook for dogsitting."

Fred brought Emma home in a taxi; the ride from the hospital to Crown Heights seemed to last forever, and they were met at the end by Emma's small garden apartment. A Christmas tree took up a large portion of one corner. A tabby cat slept beneath it, the lights turning its fur green and red. Fred trailed behind her as she walked through the house, turning on lights. She opened a kitchen drawer and pulled out a takeout menu.

"Should we order Thai?" she asked.

During the skin biopsy he'd done nothing unprofessional; he seemed to have avoided an ethical crisis that would have hurt his career. But then he'd thought about her every day for the past two weeks and had wanted very badly to see her.

"I know it must seem weird, that no one was with me at the hospital." She opened and closed the menu like an accordion. "I have friends, I just—don't like to bother them with this kind of thing. I don't want to be the sick friend."

"You are sick, though. You've been sick a while."

Emma clenched the takeout menu. "Why are you only nice to me at the clinic?"

He knew she was right. When they were alone, he was chilly and perturbed; at the clinic, pleasant and superficial. He missed the excitement of what would come next with her. He took one step, and then, quickly, he crossed the room and took the menu from her hands. Her head came up to his chin, and she pressed her forehead into his chest.

"Come over to the couch," he said. "You're supposed to be resting."

Emma woke the next morning and Fred had already gone. She tried to work from home, but she was sick from fentanyl and filled with loneliness.

Fred didn't call. It was over, she decided. She would have to withdraw, too. She didn't understand the world he lived in. Focused only on having health insurance since her early twenties, she'd never considered having a career she was passionate about. She had pursued a normal medium-paying noncompetitive path in marketing, for a company that expected only adequate effort. Her whole life, a practical choice. With Fred she'd been ready to be impulsive for once.

She spent Christmas alone with wine, her cat on top of the refrigerator, hissing at her neighbor's dog. She was sad to see the dog go when her neighbor returned from Cleveland.

It was Dr. Castillo's orders for her to have bloodwork monthly, and in early January he called with the results and told her to make an appointment. She almost requested specifically that Dr. Chen not be present at the appointment, and she wished she had when she arrived at the office and he wasn't there.

"Where's your fellow?" she asked Dr. Castillo, sitting before his collection of clocks.

He looked at her, surprised, as though he'd forgotten she and Fred had ever met. "Oh, Dr. Chen. He can tell all he needs to know from your bloodwork."

In her chest the gold-threaded feeling of being right wove itself together, crochet that crept up over her heart. With effort she kept her face neutral though her pulse tripped once before righting itself. She straightened a crooked clock on Dr. Castillo's desk. It was a bright red apple with the face embedded in its flesh.

"Please don't touch," he said.

"Sorry."

"Good news first. I was happy with the biopsy. It showed there is very little damage to the kidneys so far. But, looking at your bloodwork, the results are suboptimal. Your complements are still low, DNA high, protein in the urine still very high, which means the drugs haven't been working. Now, studies show you have the best chance of avoiding long-term kidney disease if inflammation goes down in the first year after treatment begins. We want to avoid dialysis or transplant, but we've got some time before I'll get worried. I was telling Dr. Chen that I'm content, but I want to be over the moon."

"Okay," she said.

"Let's increase the dose of mycophenolate and lisinopril and—how much prednisone are you on?"

"Five milligrams," she said.

"Good. We'll keep it there." He scanned her test results, pausing somewhere and blinking at the screen.

"Did you have a little too much Christmas cheer?"

"Excuse me?" Emma asked.

"Your liver enzymes are elevated." Dr. Castillo scrolled through her history. "But they've never been a problem before."

"Oh, I see." Emma wondered if Fred had seen the results, and what he thought. "I may have had a few more drinks than usual. Because of the holidays."

"That's fine," Dr. Castillo said. "You had a merry Christmas. A little too much at the holidays is fine. You know what to do?"

Emma remembered a time before she'd come to New York when all her doctors were women. She'd been happier then, or maybe just younger.

"Lab work," she said. "And make my next appointment on my way out."

Fred waited for Emma to leave Dr. Castillo's office. He followed her to the lab and stopped in the doorway. She sat in the phlebotomist's chair, her jacket off and arm held flat for the needle. He'd stayed awake after she'd fallen asleep in her apartment and as he thought about staying the night, the same doubts clambered up his throat. He'd ruined his chances with Emma and nearly ruined his fellowship. If he didn't leave, and fast, he'd be crossing a line far past all the ones he'd already crossed. If he stayed, he would have to call Dr. Castillo first thing in the morning, a call that could end in a request for his resignation.

The phlebotomist asked what he needed.

"Can I have some tubes for research?" He held up a biohazard bag, plump with six tubes, and a cup. "And some urine."

The phlebotomist looked at Emma.

"Sure," Emma said, watching the needle as it pierced her inner arm. The phlebotomist waved Fred's vials over, and he stood near Emma while her blood pooled in each tube. The tissue of her inner arm was scarred from all the blood she'd given in her life, a thousand vials or more, month after month after month.

"Do you need juice?" the phlebotomist asked as the tubes mounted into a pile.

Emma shook her head. "No."

"Bring this one back to me." The phlebotomist handed her a urine cup and sanitary wipe. "And this one back to him."

Fred followed her into the hallway. "It's probably easiest just to pee in one cup," he said, "and then divide it."

"I know." She disappeared into the bathroom.

Fred had spent long holiday plane rides thinking. At home in California he'd come to believe there were options. He wasn't really her physician. Dr. Castillo was in his seventies, bound to retire someday. Only a month had passed since things became complicated. Only the two of them would ever know. He hoped she had taken time to think, too, and to decide if he was worth putting their beginning behind them.

Emma returned to his side, holding two cups of yellow urine, full of the protein they were trying to get rid of.

"This one's yours," she said. He opened a plastic bag and she dropped it inside.

"There's one more thing," he said, following her out into the waiting room. "The mental health questionnaire—would you do a follow-up? We like to have data for post-biopsy."

Emma took the clipboard and checked the form's boxes. How depressed.

How anxious. How hopeful. Somewhat. Very. Only a little.

When she finished, she handed the clipboard back to him and smiled. He expected her to say something. He waited, giving her the chance to speak first. But she turned away. She'd already said her last words to him—the last real words—and he couldn't remember what they were.

"Emma."

His voice captured the attention of a woman waiting to be called for her appointment. Emma stopped, turned around, eyebrows raised. She had her phone in her hands, she was texting someone, maybe her next Tinder date.

"You need something more?" she asked.

"I was thinking—what if you went to Weill Cornell, or Columbia?"

"You didn't call."

"That's not—" he began, but she held up a hand to stop him.

"You were right not to call," she said. "You were right all along."

"I was wrong. It took me time to realize."

Emma laughed, laughter that coursed through her like a shriek through a downpour. *Maybe one day we'll laugh about it,* Fred had said weeks ago. But one day wasn't in time. She'd wanted to laugh from the beginning.

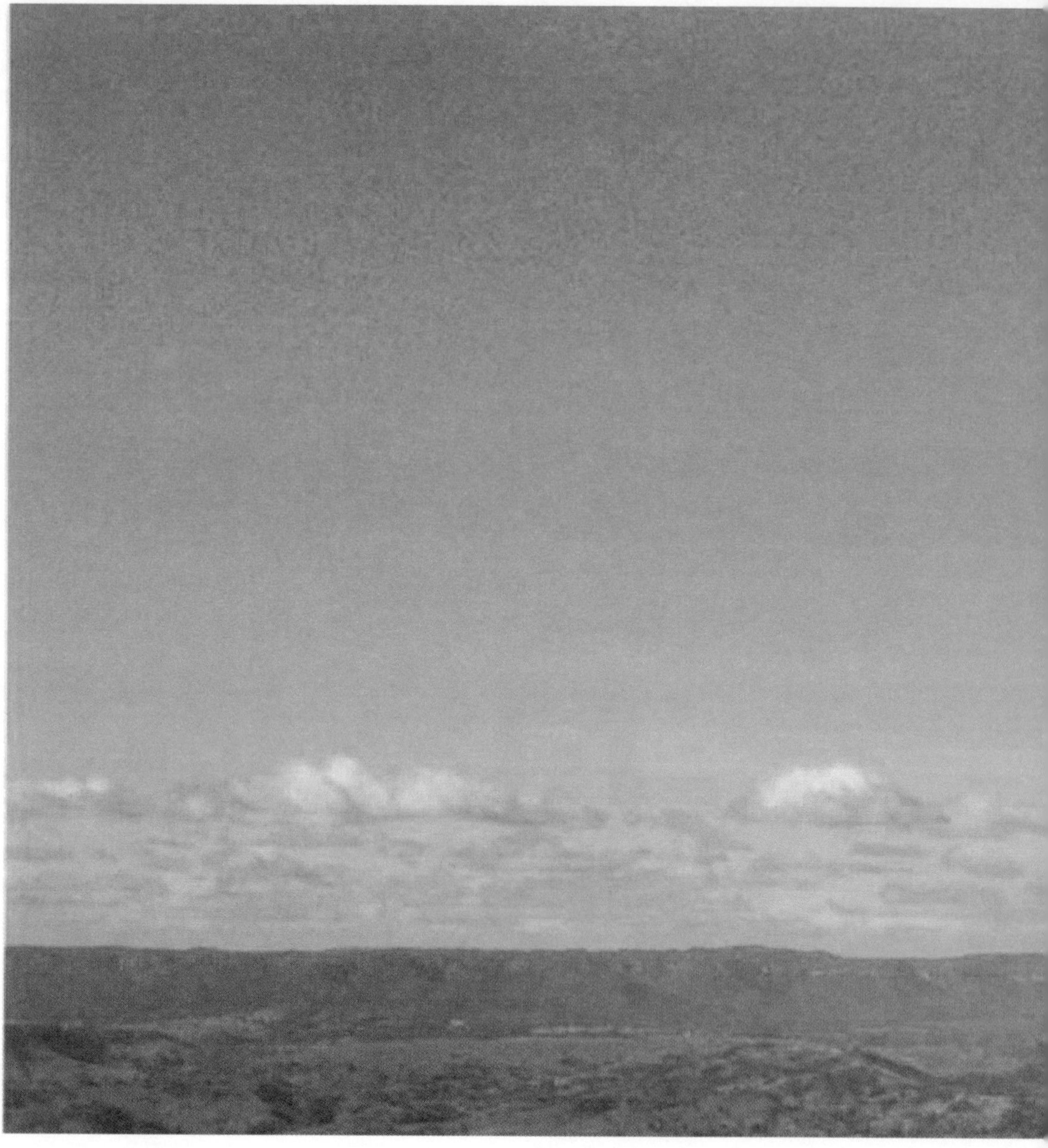

Rosemary Laing, *Flight Research #6*

[THIS AUTUMN EVENING]
KIMIKO HAHN

a golden shovel after Richard Wright

Filled with constellations, **this**
sky is clear as cold these **autumn**
months, now frozen to **evening.**
Afflicted with ice **is**
this hearth. And a room **full**
of childhood rhymes. My verses were **of**
drafts under the door, of **an empty**
yard, deciduous and pine, of a **sky**
stricken with twigs. Oh, **and one**
whiff of wind. To see **empty**
I'll return for dinner across the **road.**

[HAVING APPOINTED ALL]
KIMIKO HAHN

a golden shovel after Richard Wright

In bedtime stories, a girl, **having**
taken flight, having been **appointed**
to stay in flight, gathers **all**
the rain she can in her pockets, then **the**
snow in her satchel. She calls to the **stars**
so they will correspond **to**
her plaintive poems. **Their**
point is plain: not to flicker in the same **places**
for more than a few seconds each **summer**—
then to roll across the black heaven and **wind**
over the horizon when the moon **sleeps.**

[I AM PAYING]

KIMIKO HAHN

a golden shovel after Richard Wright

I am searching for sublet signs, **I am**
circling classified ads. **Paying**
for another rebound. **Rent**
will be the least for leave-taking, **for**
my own peeling walls, for **the**
infested linoleum, the **lice**
on sheets, in sweaters, **in**
my hair. Here, perhaps **my**
chambers—the muscled one, the **cold**
one—will please freeze. In our **room**
I looked for keepsakes. **And**
a reason to stay put. **The**
dog? No. Maybe, the **moonlight**
across the dog. And the man's back, **too.**

STRANGE ANIMAL FACTS
ADAM CLAY

I read about a species of ants that crawl
into electronics to feed on the wiring
and ultimately electrocute themselves. Upon
dying, the ants release a chemical
calling other ants to avenge their death. I shake
my phone in the early mornings
to wake it up alongside me. I walk through
the hallway of my house and think
nothing of the mechanics
of my body. I started crying yesterday
because of a single note in a song
that was mostly unremarkable
up until that moment. Later, I poured
myself down the drain with the water
I take every night habitually and ritually
to place on the nightstand and never drink.
I divide the day into parts that make sense,
but it's all meaningless to the trees growing
always for a life beyond my own. I sleep
under a blanket that resists the movement
of my body. I arrange my day
around the unnecessary and the good.

I DON'T SLEEP AT NIGHT

SAMIRA NEGROUCHE
TRANSLATED FROM THE FRENCH BY NANCY NAOMI CARLSON

I don't sleep at night when light falls.

When darkness falls, dust rises over me, tenacious dust invading my nostrils and settling, thick, on everything serving as companions.

I don't sleep at night. When silence falls, faces resurface in my memory, also those I've never seen.

———

Faces are rooted inside me, all that passed by me during the day and others I haven't seen pass by.

———

I don't sleep at night, my ears are so sensitive, they hear all the din of the day and, at night, they regurgitate the sounds, they interpret them.

Each sound must resume its place in silence. I arrange them by thickness and color, also by effects . . . it's not very scientific, it's my way of passing the time because I don't sleep. That's the story I tell, it seems more logical.

For, in fact, it's all of this that keeps me awake, the jumbled sounds I must organize when night falls, the jumbled faces deserving of a little more attention.

———

It's so sad—or so something, I can't think of the word, there's no exact word—to not greet a passing face with dignity, be it a crazed crowd, even crowds need to be honored, face after face, one after the other, especially crowds, that's why I don't blame the dust for burning my nostrils, it reminds me not to sleep, that my attention is incomplete, that all crowds deserve full attention.

FICTION

SKIN FADES
MATEO
ASKARIPOUR

Kurri tapped on the shop's glass, looking over his shoulder, hopping from left foot to right and back. Even when Titus appeared and made his way toward the front, Kurri kept *tap-tap-tapping*.

Titus turned the dead bolt, opened the door, and stood at the threshold. Kurri's eyes ping-ponged every which way.

"Morning, Titus," he said.

"Morning, Kurri. Sky falling today?"

The younger man swallowed, looked at the speckled concrete, then up, squinting. "Think I'll keep it up for now, but no promises.

Eventually, it's gotta come crashing down."

"Would a blueberry donut and a cup of extra-black coffee help?" Titus stepped aside, gestured for Kurri to enter. "Breakfast's on the bench."

Kurri ate. Titus inspected the shop. The hardwood gleamed; the artificial leather chairs shone; and Atlas's, Cassian's, and Gil's stations were immaculate. Combs resting in their Barbicide, capes hung, clipper wires untangled, blade disposal containers empty, hand mirrors spotless, straight razors folded, Clubman Pinaud powder ready to protect and smooth at a moment's notice.

Titus checked the wall clock. 8:16. "Showtime."

One last sip of coffee, and Kurri was in the chair. Titus removed a white neck strip from its dispenser and stretched and wrapped it around Kurri's thick neck. He pulled a gold cape from its wall knob, carefully draping and snapping it closed in the back.

Titus placed his hands on his young friend's shoulders, stared into the mirror. His gentle fingertips turned Kurri's head toward the mirror.

"What do you see?"

Kurri rocked his jaw, jutted out his lips, and lowered his eyes.

"Don't do that, Kurri. Don't ever do that. Look again."

"I don't like what I see, Titus," he said, staring into his lap. "That … that ain't me."

"What's the name of my shop?"

"Soul Deep," he whispered.

"What? Speak up."

"Soul Deep," he said, louder.

"That's right. Soul Deep. And you, my brother, got a soul that shines brighter than any of those flashy actors in GQ. You understand what I'm trying to tell you?"

Only when Kurri finally gazed upon himself did Titus grab his clippers, attach a number one, and begin trimming at the base of Kurri's neck, working his way around and up with a master landscaper's precision. To him, his clients' heads were a field of dreams from which their highest selves would sprout.

Once Kurri's head was smooth and uniform, Titus combed Kurri's beard, careful not to yank the hair from his skin. Kurri, eyes closed, smiling now, hummed a tune Titus didn't know. In no time, Kurri's beard, once matted and clumped like sheep wool, was now short enough to be even and just long enough to hide his more prominent scars. Over the months, he'd told Titus about their origins, cataloging each one with the fervor of a collector, but also with a strange degree of distance, as if he were only a character in a play.

"This long thunderbolt on my forearm is from a man at the shelter who wanted my dinner. Cut me in the night with a sharpened screwdriver. Just stabbed and yanked. The moon-shaped one above my lip is from a cop who tried forcing me up out the subway in the dead of winter. Man, it was colder than you ever thought cold could be. Told him I either stay down here, or the sky fall up there, you choose. Gave me a moon as a Christmas gift."

"And what did you give them in return, Kurri?" Titus once asked, hoping, in a way, that he had struck back, at least once. Just to show that every single being is capable of resistance. But when Kurri only spread his lips as wide as they could go, his teeth—some cracked, others missing, a few standing defiant—Titus understood that despite all of Kurri's talk of the sky falling, vengeance didn't dwell in him as it did in so many others.

Now, Kurri opened his eyes, roaming across his face's newly revealed geography in the mirror; Atlantis, a sunken city of riches, brought to the surface.

Titus, standing behind him, lowered his head next to Kurri's. "You see it now, right?" He grabbed a green spray bottle, "HEAVEN'S ELIXIR" scribbled in thick black Sharpie across a white piece of tape. "Latest concoction. Alcohol without the sting. You ready?" Titus *sp-sp-sprayed* the colorless mist over Kurri's forehead, nose, cheeks, and closed mouth.

One cautious eye opened, then the other. "You are a genius, Titus."

Titus looked over at the wall clock. 8:37. "All right, my friend." He removed the cape, wiped down the seat. "Let's get to it."

Kurri jumped up, unlocked the door, and grabbed a broom and a dustpan, already collecting his own discarded hair and dead skin. *Parts of himself,* Titus thought as he watched Kurri sweeping with a wide, gap-toothed smile, *gladly forgotten.*

By 10:30, Titus had cut two people, Cassian one, Gil one, Atlas none.

"Slow day," Gil said, holding to that very American tradition of stating the obvious. He wiped his brand-new sneakers free of hair. Despite being fifty-two years old and a barber, he insisted on wearing Jordans to work, especially if they were new. He did maintain the physique of an all-star college football recruit, though, so maybe he knew something the rest of them didn't. "It's

Friday," Atlas responded. "Couple years ago, people would be in here literally shoulder to shoulder." Horn-rimmed glasses, a meticulously maintained afro, and old leather shoes, Atlas was more of a "fine wine only becomes better with time" type of guy. "That damn new shop around the corner," Cassian grumbled. "Anyone check it out?" At forty-nine, he was the youngest of the bunch, but wore Mr. Rogersesque cardigans like he wanted to get old age in a choke hold long before it ever laid its fingers on him. "Love leads to loyalty," Titus said. "Y'all have been cutting with me for decades, you know that. The neighborhood changes, but people don't. So long as we continue to do our best, our best will support us." He nodded toward the window. A man wearing a white tank top and khaki slacks looked both ways, crossed the street, and approached the shop.

Rupie opened the door and gunned it for Titus's seat. "Kurri," he said, nodding. "Atlas," he repeated, nodding again. Then, "Cassian" and "Gil," both receiving nods before he looked up at Titus behind him. "Clipper God."

"I was just telling these fine gentlemen that customers crave quality, Roop. And then you show up, proving my point. Thank you, brother."

"Well," Rupie said, twisting the gold rings that adorned each of his fingers before Titus draped the cape over him, "can't say I completely agree, T."

Titus carefully removed Rupie's glasses, placing them on his station. "What do you mean?"

"How do you think I can afford to be here, getting a haircut at ten thirty-nine in the morning?"

"Isn't Silas watching the shop?"

"Silas? Man . . ." Rupie said, shaking his head. "Had to let him go. Reason I can come here and sit in your heavenly seat is because I know, for a fact, that no customers are coming in."

"What do you mean? 'Gold never gets old.' That's your motto."

"You don't see it?" he said, swiveling his chair around to face the men. "These days, my customers don't want quality, affordable jewelry. They want 'bust downs,' blinged-out chains that touch their toes, and blood diamonds practically weeping for Sierra Leone. I can't compete. At this rate, I'm not making rent next month, and that's it for me."

"The neighborhood's changing a little, Roop, but people don't. Gold is gold. Silver is silver. You'll—"

"AP. IG. VVS. You get what I'm saying?"

"Not at all."

"These young jewelers give rappers free jewelry, like an Audemars Piguet watch. These APs have diamonds that are 'very very slightly included' quality, meaning they have few internal inclusions and external blemishes. 'VVS.' And where do these jewelers and rappers show off their catastrophic creations? Instagram. 'IG.' You know what that is, right?"

"Heard of it, sure."

"Heard of it? Hell, we're being murdered by it, T. Old-timers like us are out of time. Nobody cares about classic anymore. Nobody wants substance. It's flash, flash, bang, bang. Then they're on to the next fad that 28 Savage, 36 Cent, and Coast Malone sets."

"21 Savage, 50 Cent, and Post Malone," Gil said. "Gotta know the enemy to defeat the enemy."

Titus, unfazed, got to work. Rupie was already bald, but black stubble covered his crown, so a straight razor was the way to go. Tension vibrated in his friend's every fiber; Titus's fingers, like lips to a snakebite, tried their best to suck, spit, suck, and spit their way to some sense of salvation.

"Julius coming by later," Titus said. "Made an appointment last week."

He paused and looked up at the photos on his wall. Julius as a toddler, getting his first haircut at Soul Deep; he'd wailed like a fire truck when his mother sat him on the kid cushion, but once Titus's fingers touched his head, he stopped. Another of teenage Julius, laughing as friends surrounded him, watching him get the cleanest fade of his life before taking headshots. An autograph across the bottom said "To Uncle Titus, your Famous Fade got me my big break! Love you, Julius." Whether it was true or not didn't matter, but, Titus conceded, he did begin booking bigger and bigger roles after that cut. And more young men flooded Soul Deep, begging for the "Famous Fade" they saw on *Concrete Heart*, then *Jumping Hope*, then, of course, *The Mailman's Brother*, the film that won Julius an Academy Award—Titus had been on set in Minnesota, ensuring Julius was clean for every scene.

But *Bent, Not Broken* was his favorite, in which Julius played a golf player who, despite a career-ending knee injury followed by a tabloid divorce—his wife not only cheating on him with his accountant but embezzling millions while he was in the hospital—practiced every day, eventually doing what even Tiger Woods had never done: winning the modern era Grand Slam. His final putt of the last tournament, the entire crowd as silent as deep space, then erupting like Pompeii, always made Titus cry.

There were other people on the wall. Celebrities who came in with Julius; local people whom Titus made sure would see themselves among these public figures and know that they, too were stars; a shot of himself, his father demonstrating to five-year-old Titus how to properly hold scissors, apply shaving cream, reminding him that "a haircut only lasts a week or two, son. But that feeling you give someone, of confidence and self-love, will sustain them far longer."

Rupie sighed. "Too bad Julius doesn't wear jewelry." Titus sprayed him with Heaven's Elixir, stood back, and laughed when Rupie braced for the sting that never arrived. "That alcohol?"

"New recipe. No sting."

"Wow. You're like the George Washington Carver of barbers, T," he said, scrutinizing his reflection in the mirror. "Julius coming by with his girlfriend? That singer?"

"I like her," Cassian said. "Young, but got an old voice. Aretha-like."

"Who knows," Titus said. He looked at the wall clock. 10:53. "Almost eleven. Gotta leave for a doctor's appointment at eleven fifteen, then I'll be back for Julius after that." He rarely left the shop like this, but it was the only time he could get an appointment.

Rupie removed his wallet, but Titus held up his hand. "This one's on the house."

His clean-shaven friend shot his eyes at him. "You know me, Titus. Not one for charity."

"Good, because I'm in the market for a bracelet, or something. I'll swing by later and you take the cut off the gold."

Rupie continued to stare at him, something loud and unspoken expanding between them. Then he nodded, bid the other barbers and Kurri goodbye, and left.

"Y'all hold down the fort," Titus said. He stepped outside, felt the warm sun tickle his face, and headed south.

"Afternoon, Titus," Amara said, standing in the doorway of her African braiding shop.

"Amara," Titus said, bowing. "What're you up to?"

She waved her hand in front of her face, swatting invisible flies. "Passing the time." Tall, head immaculately wrapped in gold-and-blue fabric, she crossed her arms, sucked her teeth. "Never been a problem to have five, six braiding shops on this block before. But now?" Amara looked to the left and right. "We're dropping like diseased cows. Even with lower prices."

"It'll get better. And I'll be sure to put the word out to customers that the best braider in the whole country happens to own a shop right next to my own."

At that, she finally smiled, her shoulders shaking with laughter. "One of one, Titus. You are one of one."

He nodded to the Muslim men on the sidewalk selling beanies, T-shirts, bandanas, and calling cards atop plastic tables outside of their nondescript mosque.

"Yes, brother," they said.

Up the street, a man sitting on a blue cooler held out his fist, and Titus's was there to meet it. "Coconut for you today, Titus?"

"Not now, Cecil. But have one ready for me on the way back, yeah? A big one, with lots of jelly."

The neighborhood changes, but people don't, he thought again, looking around at the intersection of his street and the main avenue. New shops, sure. A couple new people, okay. But the same ones remained, and with them came respect, admiration. The type of goodwill accrued with years of hard work and interest.

You couldn't discount a smile's return on investment, how asking after someone's ailing mother overseas would light up their insides, bulbs for eyes, incandescence shooting out their mouths, all because they and their loved ones weren't forgotten. That time you cut every local elementary school student's hair for free because there was a lice outbreak one state over. Goodwill, he told himself as he crossed the avenue, waving to a group of women pushing strollers, is everything.

He stepped aside to let an elderly man exit the building that housed a handful of doctors' offices, then entered through the sliding doors. "Morning, Mr. Oak," the building receptionist said. "You can go on up."

"Thank you, Janeisha." He walked toward the elevator but stopped. "Oh," he said, turning around. "How's your brother?"

She looked up from her computer, gave a weary smile. "Adjusting, you know. The world's changed since he went in."

"Well why don't you tell him to come by the shop and I'll catch him up on the last decade?"

Before she could stop it, she snorted and brought a hand to her mouth. "He'd love that, Mr. Oak. Thank you."

In the elevator, he found himself whistling that tune Kurri had been humming. Kurri, he thought, was a gift of a human. People had cautioned Titus against giving him a job, but in their months of working together, Kurri'd never had one serious outburst. At this rate, he'd earn enough in a couple of months to move out of the shelter, maybe get in contact with that daughter of his he sometimes spoke about. Yes, Titus said to himself, the metallic doors opening, I'll set him up with a small apartment near the shop, make sure he gets some good used furniture but a brand-new coffee machine, a couple framed photographs of the sky for the wall. He could always look at it and remember that he was the sole reason it didn't fall. So what if it was a delusion? We all had them.

"Go on in, Mr. Oak," Dr. Dixon's office manager said.

"Thank you, Tanya."

Almost as soon as he sat, Dr. Dixon entered the exam room, a large envelope in her hand.

"Mr. Oak. How are we today?"

"Good to see you, Dr. Dixon. All's wonderful, thank you. How are you?"

"No serious complaints. Daughter got into Yale, so the whole family's up in arms."

"Why's that?"

"We're Harvard people." She closed her eyes, as if experiencing a brief headache.

"Ah," he said, nodding. "Had a cousin's son go to Dartmouth, but I'm still not sure what the problem is."

"Harvard and Yale are like the Lakers and the Celtics, Mr. Oak. So long as they stand, so will their rivalry. I mean, my husband was literally in tears. She's always been rebellious, but this is something else, you know?"

"Sounds like she's just coming into her own. She'll get there, and when she does, you, your husband, and the whole family will be proud of what you've made."

"I hope so," she said, removing an x-ray from the envelope and holding it up.

"That me?"

"It is. Well, your hand. Let me ask you a question: Does it ache anywhere?"

Titus laughed. "It aches everywhere."

She pointed to the scan. "I ask because as you'll see here," circling what looked like a dog's rawhide chew toy, "there's serious joint damage in the wrist and fingers. In both hands. It's very common in men your age." Dr. Dixon rested the scan on a counter and looked into his eyes. "But it is degenerative, Mr. Oak. Unfortunately, this means you'll need to slow down at work."

Titus held his hands up, flipping them over and back. He thought about how he'd had these hands his entire life. Before he took his first breath, they were with him. They were the hands his father held, placing a safety razor into his palm, instructing him on how to hold the skin taut while shaving a man. These hands made people's souls sing through their skin. Hands that held Glorietta's hands, when they first courted and then when she got sick. The same hands that fed baby Birdie, that struggled against teenage Birdie's sharpening bones, that touched her frozen face in that Los Angeles morgue after the drugs ate her up.

"These hands?" he asked, still holding them in front of him.

"I'm not saying you need to stop cutting altogether, just a bit less. If you don't slow down," she said, "it'll only get worse. God forbid your fingers ache as you're holding a straight razor to someone's throat? Flinch from pain with a pair of sharp scissors in your hand? You cut children, don't you?"

"Julius," he said, his voice coming out more like a whine than he wished. "You know who Julius Goodman is, right?"

She placed a hand on his shoulder and laughed. "You only talk about him every time I see you, Mr. Oak. But even if you didn't, of course. Between the movies and advertisements, you can't escape him. They say he's Hollywood's new leading man."

"I'm cutting his hair today. In"—he looked up at the wall clock. 11:36––"less than an hour. I've already cut three people today, but I can't not cut Julius's hair, can I?"

Her smile flattened. "Of course not, Mr. Oak. How about this? Moving forward, you do only two cuts a day, and we start physical therapy in the next week or two. You can leave the long lines of people begging for a haircut to your younger barbers, hmm?"

His eyes fell to his lap, where his treacherous hands lay. He could imagine them turning to stone, digit by digit, until his blood became concrete and he moved like the Tin Man. "Two cuts a day?"

"Two cuts a day."

Titus inhaled, grateful that his lungs were still intact, more grateful, in this moment, for all of the arteries and bodily processes he couldn't name, but which carried on all the same in unconditional service of him standing, sitting, laughing, dancing, sighing, living, and, yes, he now thought, even dying. These bones of mine, this blood of mine.

"Deal."

When he exited the elevator, Janeisha was on the phone but still gave him a parting wink. He winked back, walked through the doors, and felt his pocket vibrate. He brought out his phone, his heart rising when he saw it was Julius, swan diving when he read the text. "Can't make it today. Sorry, Unc. Can you get me when I'm back in town next week?"

Next week? Titus's hands were ready for him now. No matter, he'd rest and soak them in hot water. He would put every ounce of goodwill into these hands of his, so that after this next cut, Julius would look in the mirror and see himself as a future great; the type that when people said "Julius," no last name was needed, just like Sidney, Denzel, and Morgan.

"It's a plan, Stan," Titus replied.

Well, he thought, crossing the avenue again, head held high. This is a new beginning. Titus decided to take the long way back to the shop, moving westward. He turned right on the next avenue and noticed a group of people huddled in front of a shop window, peering in. When he came upon them, he looked up, saw a sign that said "Blade Ready," a barber pole spinning beside it. This must be that new shop Cassian was cursing earlier, he thought.

The mass of people made it hard to see inside, but when a few shorter kids jostled in front of him, he had a clear view of Julius, in a barber chair, nodding, laughing, and speaking as a young barber, with some lamp attached to his head like he was mining for coal, cut, ducked, cut, and ducked again as if some invisible hand attached to Julius's head was punching him.

Titus watched as another barber held what looked like a gun with some sort of alcohol-filled tank, mist coming out through a barrel lit neon blue. Hip-hop played so loudly he was sure they couldn't hear each other, and it even seemed as though the shop doubled as a dispensary in the back; a glass counter displayed colorful candies, RAW rolling papers, and other reefer paraphernalia he didn't recognize.

Before he knew it, he was inside, standing in front of Julius, struggling to absorb the impact of whatever had just crashed into him.

"Aye, wait outside, my man," Julius's barber said. "Walk-ins gotta wait a couple hours. Better to make an appointment."

Julius froze when he looked up and saw Titus. "Unc…"

Titus held out his hand, one of the two that had betrayed him. "It's okay, it's okay. I know there's a good explanation. Just tell me what it is."

"This your uncle for real, J?" the barber asked.

"Lemme holla at him for a second, Curtis, aight?" Julius said.

Julius got up, towering over Titus and his barber, removed his cape, and gestured for Titus to follow him to a room in the back. Inside were two leather couches, a TV with some gaming console attached, a stocked refrigerator, poker table, and full bar.

"Julius. Just explain."

"Look, Unc. You can't cut me anymore."

Now, Titus thought, his ears were betraying him, too. Maybe even his brain, short-circuiting to the point that his robot-like eye-twitching, nose-wrinkling, and lip-biting must have resembled some sort of stroke to Julius. But Julius only continued, asking Titus, "You've cut me how many times over the last year?"

"Six. Every time you've come into town."

"And after every time, I've had to come here, to Curtis, to get it cleaned up."

"What do you mean?"

"I leave your chair with loose hairs circling my mouth, nicks in the corners of my forehead. The shape-ups aren't as straight as the younger cats', and"—he paused, shaking his head—"it kills me to say this, but your Famous Fade ain't so famous these days. The blending's off, like some teenage girl who just discovered makeup. I can't have that, Unc. I'm out here with TMZ trying to kill me weekly, Wendy Williams scrutinizing my relationships, Charlamagne Tha God searching for a reason, just one"—he held up his long finger, as if Titus forgot what the number looked like—"to make me Donkey of the Day."

"Donkey of the what?"

He flung his open hands toward him. Hands that hadn't betrayed the young actor yet. "This is exactly what I'm saying, Unc. You're out of touch. And I'm at a point in my career where I'll either fly, or fade and be forgotten."

"But what about your performance in *Bent, Not Broken*? It was unforgettable."

"It has a fifty-eight percent rating on *Rotten Tomatoes*. My lowest. Trust me, I want that one to be forgotten."

Julius looked toward the closed door, then wrapped his arms around Titus's back, like he used to do when he was a kid and he couldn't believe what he saw in the mirror: who he was and could be. The day was beginning to be too much, and even if Julius had never spoken to him so bluntly, this embrace told him that there was still real love between them; that Julius remembered.

"We gotta grow, you know," Julius said, finally letting go. "Evolve. Change."

Titus wiggled his fingers, twisted his aching wrists. Humans have had the same fingers, the same wrists, the same ankles, the same hearts, the same hair for hundreds of thousands of years. You don't see children being born with hairy eyeballs, blue fingernails, or tongues with tiny ears. We've stayed the same for so long because it works. A classic model. The Neanderthals went extinct, but we're still here. I, he thought, am still here.

"How about this," Titus said. "You'll be back in town next week?"

"Yeah. Mom's birthday."

"Okay. Tell Curtis out there to cool it with the trimming, just even it all up from where you're at now. Then next week, I cut you one last time. I promise I'll make it the best haircut of your life. So flawless that you'll win another Academy Award. No, so indisputable that they'll create a new award, just for you. What do you say?"

Julius looked at Titus, his eyes seeming to search, find, and confirm an essential truth. Then, his face loosened with relief. "It's a plan, Stan. You know I'll still stop by the shop after, right? Send a couple friends your way every now and then."

Titus's feet, which were supposedly still on his side, carried him across the shiny black floor, past the barbers' raised eyebrows, amusement curling up at the corner of their lips, then finally through the throng of onlookers on the sidewalk that had only grown since he'd entered. Skin fades, he thought, but the soul doesn't. He had to believe that. Even if he were a church of one. Otherwise, what was the point?

"Titus!" someone called. "Titus, what're you doing out there staring at your feet? Come in, man."

He looked up. Somehow, he'd walked all the way around the block, looping back on the same street as Soul Deep, and was now in front of Trini Time. Through the open door, Beryl, metal serving spoon in hand, beckoned him inside.

"Afternoon, Beryl."

"Titus," she said, scooping some rice and peas into a Styrofoam box, tossing gravy on top. "Where's that double?" she called to the kitchen before turning back to him. "Titus," she repeated, shaking her head. "Why're you out there staring at your feet like a damn beh beh?"

"Just thinking. That's all."

"I've been doing a lot of thinking myself. Think it's time to go back 'ome."

He stood up straighter. "To Trinidad? But why?"

"This country has ground me down, man. Ground me down like pestle and black pepper."

"I'm sorry, Beryl."

"You know, the other day, a woman come in here," she sucked her teeth long and hard. "Titus, would you believe she was some kind of food critic? Someone come by the shop and show me an article in which this woman demeaned me, my work, this very place, calling it 'old world,' 'unhygienic,' and said for the city to come and inspect. Too much grease, too much fat, she wrote." Beryl sucked her teeth again, long and hard. "No invention. Invention? The Lord invented all of this delicious food for us to eat as we've eaten it for centuries."

She laughed, closed up the box, and slid it to the side. "Got this young girl whose grandmother is from the island," she said, lips snarling. "Opens a restaurant up the road. First day, gets a line out the door around the block. I go check it out myself. So many deliverymen zooming in and out you'd a thought she was FedEx. She looks so *nice*, so *clean* behind the register. No apron, because she doesn't do any of the cooking herself! I go up to her and say, 'lemme get a saltfish buljol.' When I get it, I say, 'Where the scotch bonnet?' She say, 'These people don't like scotch bonnet.' I'm done, Titus. I'm d-o-done."

"Try and hold on, Beryl," he said, hands in front of him, moving in time with his words. When he noticed, he dropped them to his side, putting them in time out. "Don't leave just yet."

"What for?"

"That young woman's shop probably won't be here in a year, and then the neighborhood will come back to you. They'll yearn for the authentic taste and praise you for maintaining it. Goodwill is everything."

"Listen, friend. Goodwill can't buy groceries. Might get me credit, but debt is debt. These young ones are straight Machiavellian. No care in the world, about anything, except what they see fit to call victory: the annihilation of the past and the people they view as its representatives. Us."

A man walked in, Beryl greeted him, took his money, and handed him the Styrofoam box. When he left, Titus smiled and said, "See?" She just shook her head at him, and a strange feeling began to unfurl in him then, driving him home instead of back to Soul Deep, up his brownstone's steps, through the heavy wooden door, and directly into his armchair, broken in by a decade of sitting.

He turned on the television, National Geographic playing a program about poisons found in nature and their contemporary uses, when his phone vibrated. It was Atlas.

"Everything okay? We're getting worried."

"I'm not feeling too well, Atlas. Don't want you all to catch it, so think I'm going to stay home for the next week."

"Oh," he said. "Can I get you anything? Do you have food?"

"Yeah, I'm okay. But when you open up, could you please grab Kurri a blueberry donut and extra-black coffee? Helps him ease into the day, and I don't want to break the routine. I'll settle up his pay when I'm back."

"Of course, Titus. We'll take care of him."

"Why are you so comfortable with growing old, Atlas?"

The line went quiet, and Titus thought they'd been disconnected, but then, "Because old age isn't a curse, Titus. It's a gift. A gift that not everyone lives to receive."

He stayed there, in that armchair, in front of that TV, with National Geographic playing, for hours. If this were a movie, this would be the part where the film would employ a fast-forward effect, showing the TV's light fluttering over Titus's hard, unmoving face; him passing out, waking up, eating bowls of cereal, going to the bathroom, sitting back in the armchair.

At some point, the channel would change, and he'd see Julius's bright eyes, chiseled jaw, and extraordinary smile staring back at him: the final scene from *Bent, Not Broken*, when he sinks the ball, throws up his arms, and the crowd, like Old Faithful, bursts into incredulous applause. No one, except his coach, who'd died in the previous scene, had believed in him. Not even the character himself. This time, for the first time, Titus wouldn't cry. But his phone battery would die, the sun would fall, rise, fall, and rise through the living room's window, and there would be Titus, not in a movie, but shifting, breathing, and thinking. However, Titus's life didn't fast-forward for days; it slowed down to an almost imperceptible crawl. Finally, his mind's clouds only slightly clearer, he rose on Thursday and walked into Rupie's jewelry shop.

"T?" Rupie said, rounding the glass display case, grabbing his friend's arm. "T, you okay? Atlas said you've been sick. And, man, you look horrible."

"AP. IG. VVS. I get it now, Roop. I finally get it."

"You get what, T? I was just frustrated."

"I feel like I'm disappearing, Roop. Like I'm literally fading in front of my own eyes. Cell by cell. Atom by atom. Can you believe people call Beryl's food 'old world'?"

"What? Come." He guided Titus to a chair, went in the back and returned with a cold bottle of water.

"Roop." He looked up at him. "Doesn't it sometimes feel like life is just one long fade? That everything just blends together until it disappears? I know you know what I mean."

"Hey," Rupie said, grabbing Titus's shoulder. "How did it go with Julius last week? I didn't see the usual crowd at the shop."

"I'm going to cut him tomorrow," Titus replied, inhaling. "Think it'll be our last."

"Well, that's just how it goes sometimes. Won't change the past, though." He ran his hand over his stubbly head, stared down at Titus. "You still want that gold?"

"Actually, I came for something else. Found some of Glorietta's old jewelry I want to clean. Gold. Got anything for that?"

"KCN. Potassium cyanide. But you don't want to go messing with that, Titus. Bring the gold over here and I'll take care of it. Call it even from the last cut."

Titus twisted his neck toward the door, watched a bus pass, people coming and going. "This is something I'd like to do on my own, Roop. If that's okay."

Giving up, Rupie waved Titus toward the back, showing him the granular, sugar-like substance. He demonstrated how to properly mix it, dip the gold, then remove and clean it free of oxidation. "You know this is illegal? Just clean the jewelry and bring the rest of this back to me, plus the used solution in a glass container. There are rules around this stuff. Hazardous waste."

"Will do, Roop. Thank you."

"Why don't you come over Sunday night? Me, you, Amara, and even Beryl will have a get together like old times. Beer, food, dominoes, dancing. My cousin in Guyana just sent me this El Dorado vintage rum. Twenty-five years old. You hear me? Two five. And worth seven hundred dollars."

"We'll see, Roop. That okay?"

"Sure it is, T." He pointed to the baggie still in Titus's hand. "Be careful with that stuff."

Titus stared through the window of Soul Deep across the street. Gil and Atlas each had a customer, Cassian was cleaning his station, and Kurri was sweeping cut hair and dead skin. He'd never contemplated the day he'd slow down cutting hair, or stop altogether; he figured he'd cut hair until his last breath. A question fluttered across his mind: If I am not the thing I do and am known for, who am I? What am I? Seeing his friends carry on as usual, he felt a sense of weightlessness. The shop would go on until it didn't. Gil, Atlas, and Cassian would keep cutting, until they didn't. And Kurri, Kurri would keep sweeping, until he didn't. One day, maybe he'd even figure out how to really make the sky fall. Maybe the world would teach him that you actually can't kill a man, or stop the ticking of time, with kindness.

Back home, he ate, cleaned the living room, then got to work with the KCN. In the morning, he fried two eggs, dipping toast into the runny yolks, and sipped a cup of coffee as he read the newspaper. He sat there, staring at the solution he'd poured into a plastic bottle; "HEAVEN'S ELIXIR II" written on a piece of white tape across its front. Around noon, Julius texted him.

"Taking mom out for lunch now, Unc. Flight at 8 tonight. Can you meet me at my hotel around 4? It's the new Sunrise Hotel downtown."

"See you then," Titus typed back.

When Titus got to the hotel, duffel bag in hand, Julius opened his room's door, a dark cloud covering his face.

"Hey, Unc."

"Hey, Julius."

"We gotta make this quick. Flight was moved up."

Titus nodded, entered the room, and began removing his supplies as Julius furiously texted on his phone.

"I just lost a role," Julius said, throwing his body into a chair. Titus attempted to wrap the white strip around his neck, but he pushed it away. "Hold on, Unc. Can't you see I'm in the middle of something? I needed this one."

Titus stood there, waiting until Julius was finished texting.

"Okay," he said, pocketing his phone. "Now drape me."

He did as he was told. Connected his clippers to the wall outlet, placed the straight razor and a fresh blade on the bed, as well as the spray bottle.

"Skin fade, Unc," Julius said, staring at himself in the mirror. "Last one, so make it perfect, okay?"

Titus nodded and turned the clippers on.

"Majoya said this was gonna happen. They always pit you against five other dudes for the role, knowing you weren't going to get it. And you can't call them out on it, either. Or else you're labeled as difficult. Majoya said if I'm not careful, I'll be pushed to the side. If she didn't perform at the Grammys last year, she might not be relevant today. 'Always gotta stay relevant,' she says."

Titus ran the clippers over the top of Julius's symmetrical head. Just from seeing the top of that head when he was a kid, Titus knew Julius was destined for more. All great men have great heads. Frederick Douglass. Nelson Mandela. Muhammad Ali. Even Sammy Davis Jr.

"Action movies are where it's at now. People don't go to the theaters for *Forrest Gump* anymore. You think *The Shawshank Redemption* would get asses in seats today? No way." He laughed, still staring at himself. "You gotta hustle differently now to become a name. Look different, too. Bigger. But they also want you humble. Real humble. They can go find someone doing a Web series on YouTube and make them a star."

"Mmhm." Titus blended the fade down to Julius's ear, running his fingers around his lower head; they still knew a uniform cut, how to work a field from which radiance grew.

"Majoya—"

"I'm hearing a lot about your girlfriend, Julius," Titus said, unconsciously harkening back to a time, only months ago, when he gave Julius advice and Julius listened. "You used to never focus on these things. The money. In *Bent, Not Broken*—"

Julius leaped up and stared the older man down. "Unc, *Bent, Not Broken* is not a masterpiece! It's not. And just because you like it doesn't mean that I need to go back to that. Do you know how insecure I was when we shot that? How scared I was? But I'm not scared anymore. You can't be."

"Action movies?" Titus said, head tilted back to meet the younger man's eyes. "There was a time when a character's arc was just as exciting as a car chase. Sidney could destroy your whole world with the twitch of his lips. You're meant for more, Julius. Much more."

Julius shook his head, sat back down, and looked at himself in the mirror again. "Just cut me, Unc."

Titus moved to Julius's mustache, bringing the straight razor to one side of his upper lip, then the other; beautiful, slanted, symmetry.

"Why did you lie to me last week, Julius?"

Julius's jaw clenched under the blade. He closed his eyes, inhaled, opened them again. Where there was once anger now floated pity. "How was I supposed to know you'd be taking a walk in the middle of the day? You never do that."

"But," Titus said, pausing with the straight razor in his hand, fluorescent hotel light bouncing off the blade. "You hurt me."

"Hurt? When I was a kid, I'd walk through Soul Deep's door, and you'd look a hundred feet tall. But now . . ." He shook his head. "Now you sound like a child, Unc. The world could be crumbling around you, and you'd say, 'Just a little rubble. We'll rebuild. And, hey, what comes next will be even better.' You're twice my age, but you still don't get it. Me? I'm not going anywhere except up."

They held each other's eyes in the mirror; souls, not skin, singing their truest songs. Blow after blow, terrible things, through the death of a wife and daughter, had tried, but never succeeded, to fell the walls Titus had fortified within his spirit. He didn't know what would happen next. But as thoughts of the future almost carried him away, he became aware of the small movement, of the nearly inaudible whirring and low thrum of electricity flowing through his fingers, and continued cutting.

STORIES OUT OF SCHOOL / ANNE P. BEATTY

LOCKDOWN DRILL

At the pre-appointed hour, I check the door, pull shades, hit lights. Should I use butcher paper to cover the glass panel on the door, or does that take too much time? We talked about it for forty minutes during a faculty meeting. Now half the teachers do it, half the teachers don't. I do. To expedite the process, I keep my roll of purple paper, dull as a bruise, behind the scarred filing cabinet with torn pieces of masking tape already on it.

My students hug their knees. We huddle in a corner. We would joke but nothing's funny. One girl points to a bookshelf's ledge, eye level for all of us. Scrawled in red marker are the words *We are all cannibals.*

"Why's it there?" she whispers. I shrug. We smile; still, nothing's funny.

Sometimes, though, my students giggle at nothing. I get it. To laugh is to be less terrified. But I have to shush them. Principals come around and bang on the doors, rattle the handles to make sure the locks hold. One principal, if he heard students talking or laughing, came in later and yelled at the students, then yelled at you in front of the students, then yelled at the students some more. Everyone must be silent.

One principal instructed all teachers to make students grab something they could use as a weapon: a stapler, a three-hole punch, a chair, legs jeering out like spikes. She came in, wild-eyed as a bucking horse, and showed students how to swing a stapler like a bat. A girl cried that day. "No weapons," I said, after the principal left. "You don't have to do that."

One year we had red cards and green cards. Slide a green card under the door if everyone is okay, red if someone is injured. *What if the shooter sees the cards and then knows people are in the room?* Another forty minutes of a faculty meeting. Now everyone has laminated cards in their drawers. No one knows if we are supposed to use them.

The year the code was "Teachers, check your email" on the intercom, half the teachers went into lockdown and the other half checked their email. We did not talk about that in a faculty meeting.

The students whisper to me about the new teacher, who is very old, and who barricaded herself behind two bookshelves during the first drill.

"With her students?" I ask.

"By herself."

The minutes tick by. Now we are all

staring at it. *We are all cannibals.*

Days later, after the "all clear," after we go back to thesis statements, after we sleep under our down-filled duvets, I will Google the sentence throbbing in my head and learn it's the title of a work by French anthropologist Claude Levi-Strauss, a book that argues, as one reviewer notes, "there's no such thing as an advanced versus a primitive society."

Philippe Halsman, *JUMP (Thomas E. Dewey)*

Philippe Halsman, *JUMP (Kim Novak)*

FICTION / UCHEOMA ONWUTUEBE

WHERE ARE YOU AND WHERE IS MY MONEY

TO: odogwu.felix
FROM: Njideka1997
SUBJECT: You Must Pay!
18TH NOVEMBER

Odogwu Felix,
   Not all men are scum. Not all men leave you on read. Not all men fail to keep to their words as they skillfully entangle you in a braid of lies, braids that rival the hairdressers' under the flyover at the main market. Not all men disappear before the crack of dawn. Some stay and offer explanations, tell you why they cannot see you again, especially when you are certain you've done them no evil. Reasonable men say when they'll pay back the money you lent them. I thought you were reasonable. I lied to myself. Where are you and where is my money?

TO: odogwu.felix
FROM: Njideka1997
SUBJECT: You Must Pay!
18TH NOVEMBER

Odogwu,
   Have you seen that 700K? You must return it. If you like, run to Kafanchan o, run to Antarctica, you will pay back every dime you took from me. If not, watch your bloodline die of a wasting disease. I type this with one hand and with the other I clutch my chest, kneeling naked under the glow of a full moon. You do not want to trifle with the curses of a pained woman. That 700K will bring you to ruin, ruin more devastating than madness. Mark my words.

TO: Njideka1997
FROM: Adanma.nwosu
SUBJECT: write his bosses
19TH NOVEMBER

Babe,

    Do you realize Christmas is coming? Smell the Harmattan and its dust, tickling the nose. The udara trees are in full bloom and soon hawkers will line the streets with trays laden with their yellow fruits, urging you to buy. You cannot go back to Umuahia empty-handed. You promised your mother a full bag of rice this time, unlike last year when you gave her only two pints. Her patience has been tried, that woman. How do you want her to feel when she sees other women in the yard showing off the bags of beans and rice, cartons of sardines, and tinned tomatoes their children gifted them? Chimee's school fees, his Christmas shoes and clothes, your mother's house rent, her shop rent. Weren't you planning on taking your mother to the university teaching hospital for her incessant chest pain? I'm certain you do not want to stand by and watch her die without her reaping the fruits of her labor. You are not the first daughter for nothing. Like the good friend that I am, I am reminding you of all this. If you had listened to me and dumped that Odogwu when he started acting like werey, this hot trouble would not have found your address. I begged you then, leave his broke ass and let me hook you up with better men, old cash cows that will spoil you with credit alerts, men who will give you their ATM cards and checkbooks for keeps, but you said you were in love. Yeye love.

    And it baffles me why you are mercy-ing for him. If I ask what you've done, you'd say you've sent him emails. Emails? Do you think this is customer service, where you use soft voice to pacify irate customers? 700,000 naira is not beans. You want to be the proverbial idler who washed his hands only to crack nuts for chickens? Even if this was runs money you earned from caressing old men, you still shouldn't let it spirit away just like that, haba! You want to give your mother a heart attack and affirm her suspicions that her enemies are outwitting her again? This is your seven months' salary we are talking about.

    Here is Odogwu's branch manager's email: <u>Onuoha.Fidelis@paracletesolutions.com</u>. Write him and call out that bastard. Fidelis is a kind man. We dated briefly but things didn't work out between us. You know these old men and their plenty palaver. I met him months ago, around the period I went to relieve Sophia during her maternity leave in our Ikoyi branch. But enough of this gist; write Fidelis. Tell him his staff is a swindler. When we were together, Fidelis mentioned he had grown daughters, so I believe he'd be touched by your plight.

Go hard on Odogwu. Forget that you love(d) him. Money is now involved so fling that dirty love out the window. Call his old mother. I don't care if she is a vegetable seller in the village. Tell her you're coming with the police if she doesn't produce her son. Call his village people if you have their numbers. Odogwu's head is not correct and we ought to treat him like the mad person he is.

TO: Onuoha.Fidelis
FROM: Njideka1997
SUBJECT: Odogwu Felix swindled me.
21ST NOVEMBER

Good day, Sir,

My name is Njideka Nwankwo. I am the assistant logistics manager at EverGreen Transport Company. We met last year at your company's Christmas party and Odogwu introduced me as his girlfriend. I also facilitate all waybill businesses for Paraclete Solutions. The last time the printer in your office broke down and was sent to the warehouse in Abuja for repairs, I was the one who ensured it arrived within twenty-four hours. The security locks you needed for your head office arrived intact because of me. Every time I see a parcel from Paraclete Solutions, I swing into action and give it top priority. Why? Because my boyfriend works there, and I am a very supportive girlfriend.

However, I am writing to ask you to please make Odogwu return my money. We were planning our lives together. This December, he was supposed to knock at the door of my people and start the customary introductions. He had even paid the rent for the house where we would build our home. All that remained was a befitting car and he needed extra cash to add to the one million naira he'd been saving. He had seen a fairly used Chrysler Sebring, last year's model, for a give-away price of N1.7 million and if he didn't act fast, he'd lose the deal. The plan was simple. He'd pay me back in three installments. Now I don't know where he is. He wouldn't take my calls for weeks and my attempts to see him have proved abortive. Last time I saw him was when he walked me to the bus park on my way to our Ilorin branch for an official assignment. He said he'd call to know if I arrived safely. I've been waiting for his call. I could be under a trailer at this moment on the dangerous highway, and he wouldn't care. His neglect has always been a bone of contention in our relationship. I returned to Lagos, gearing up to confront him for his callousness, but I found him gone. His disappearance is hardly the problem. I just want my N700,000. Please would you help me?

TO: Njideka1997
FROM: Onuoha.Fidelis
SUBJECT: Re: Odogwu Felix swindled me.
22ND NOVEMBER

Dear Miss Njideka Nwankwo,

    I wish I could remember you but I don't. Odogwu Felix had a reputation for introducing many young women as his partners. I would need the memory of a CCTV to recall the influx of women who waited for him, sitting patiently at the reception, until the close of work. Unfortunately, he no longer works with us. He resigned last week without warning. He only informed management that his time with us had come to an end. He gave no advance notice. Terrible professional behavior. Yes, he was a heedless young man but his joviality made customers smile. His friends here said he got a Canadian visa and has left the country. I'd advise you to speak to any member of his family to clarify this claim. This is also to inform you that Paraclete Solutions will not bear the liability of Odogwu Felix's debt to you. Our company policy of respecting the privacy of our staff and clients stands true. However, it is a pity you had to part with your hard-earned money this way.

    Take heart.

TO: Adanma.nwosu
FROM: Njideka1997
SUBJECT: I am finished
23RD NOVEMBER

Ada,

    Remember when we were little and after some spanking for a misdemeanor—careless hands that have broken the chinaware again, watching TV when it was time for homework—we'd sit on the balcony and cry? The balcony was a brilliant spot for the audience it availed. Neighbors would pass by and find a little girl crying and render their sympathy. And turning to our parents, they'd playfully scold, "Mummy Njide, why did you beat your little girl?"

I wish I still had that innocence; all I want to do is sit still in the middle of the road and weep. Yet some things happen to you and for shame, you dare not mourn publicly. Who do I run to for help? My mother, whose hopes rest squarely on my shoulders? I think of Chimee and the likelihood he'd be sent out of school for late school fees again and I feel like a failure.

I'm tossing in bed, willing my phone to make him call, pushing it aside when it rings and it is not Odogwu. It's midnight and my neighbor's generator has sputtered to a stop. Crickets fill the night with music. Even Chidera, the baby next door, has stopped crying, her thumb in her mouth as her tiny body succumbs to sleep. Her mother will lie down now and soon find respite on her side of the bed. Where will I find my own respite? I pace my room like one whose mind is no longer in her possession. I can hear the hooting of owls on the roof, the distant clatter of pans upset by nocturnal creatures. I have no reason to keep watch. He will not call me. I have dialed his number for the umpteenth time and the same response greets me: not available, just as everything was with him. I should have read the signs when his eyes roved and he flirted with everything in skirts. When he constantly spent money on "projects" that never took flight. I should have known. I was blinded by the need to tick all the boxes. I have done everything in my life correctly: good grades in school, a job right after graduation, supporting my mother's business. I strived to secure a steady relationship that would hopefully lead to marriage. Ada, I was winning. But look where my efforts at love have led me.

TO: Njideka1997
FROM: Adanma.nwosu
SUBJECT: You are wasting time
23RD NOVEMBER

Babe,
Why are you writing me poetry? Clatter of pots, nocturnal creatures indeed. Do you think morphing into Shakespeare or J. P. Clark will bring back your money? I know you're grieving but the earlier we take action, the better. If his

former company has washed their hands of him, then it's time to harass someone else. The list of people to arrest is long: his pastor, who is also your pastor, his friends, and most especially his mother. One of my former zaddies, Mustapha, has just been made the divisional police officer at Ubakala police station. As God would have it, Odogwu's hometown is Ubakala and his mother lives there. Just give the order and your money will resurface. Let us shake his mother up. Odogwu must have presented that money to her and knelt to receive prayers for journey mercies. You know Nigerian men constantly front as responsible adults to their parents. He must have said to his mother, "Mama, this is the fruit of my labor. Hold on to it as I go into the world and bring you more dividends." And the old woman would bless his "venison" with tears streaming down her eyes, not knowing her son is a garden-variety criminal. And in her group in church or the market, she'd brag the loudest and make other people's children seem like efulefus that don't work hard enough in the city. I know you wouldn't want to ruffle her feathers because she is elderly and perhaps prone to high blood pressure. But she is an accomplice, and her son, if he had an ounce of integrity, should have thought of her health before he swindled you. She knows where her son is, and even if she can't produce the money, she can sell a piece of family property and settle you once and for all. When you are ready to do something, write me. Until then, keep your poetry to yourself.

TO: Njideka1997
FROM: HR, EverGreen Transport and Logistics Company
SUBJECT: internal memo to njideka nwankwo on tardiness and absentmindedness
1ST DECEMBER

Miss Njideka Nwankwo,

It has come to the company's attention that you have been late to work for the past three weeks, thereby slowing down operations and the onboarding of parcels. You have also been responsible for the displacement of four top-priority packages, one of which includes a bride's wedding heirloom from her great-grandmother. You snapped at a long-standing client, Chief Omego, and he has withdrawn all his shares and investment. Your actions have cost the company hundreds of thousands of naira and have brought this month's profit margin low. You are hereby asked to reply to this memo, detailing the reasons behind this gross carelessness and recent tardiness. State why the company should not terminate your contract immediately. This memo must be responded to before the close of work today.

If this continues, nevertheless, you leave the company no option but to terminate your contract and hire other unemployed Nigerians who are willing to do your job for half your salary.

NB: Your salary will be deducted to cover the loss you have incurred for the company.

Thanks.

TO: HR, EverGreen Transport and Logistics Company
FROM: Njideka1997
RE: internal memo to njideka nwankwo on tardiness and absentmindedness
1ST DECEMBER

Dear HR,

I sincerely apologize. I am going through personal challenges that have made me inattentive. As for Chief Omego, he perpetually crosses the line of professionalism, and this time, I had to slap his hands off my cheeks. I know I should have endured as usual for the sake of our profit. However, I ran out of patience last week.

I promise to act respectfully next time. Is there a way my salary could remain undeducted? I am desperately in need of money, and I ask the company to please pardon my errors, on the grounds of previous good behavior.

TO: Amanda, Godfrey, Chidinma, Ogechi
FROM: HR, EverGreen Transport and Logistics Company
SUBJECT: I told you so!!!
1ST DECEMBER

Didn't I tell y'all Njideka isn't as smart as she portrays? Agreed, her campaign designs are data driven. She understands the language of shares and can read the toughest graphs. However, I have good knowledge that she really *really* gave all her savings to her boyfriend, Odogwu Felix. Yes, the same Felix that was doing cartwheels in my DM like the clown he is, showing his circus moves. Remember that one Friday night in October, at the BlueBird Nightclub, the bro-stitute followed me home and told me his girlfriend was just a girl he pitied and he didn't know how to break up with her.

Now, this same Odogwu carried her money and japaed to Canada. LMAOOOO. That's why she's been acting funny for weeks. The thing that'd make me give a Nigerian man my hard-earned money has not been born. Seven months' salary to a man? Dear Jesus, make it make sense. Of all men, Odogwu Felix? I see him almost every night when I go dancing with my girls. Felix changes girls the way you'd change knickers. And the way Njideka carries herself, you'd think she has common sense. Every day she wears the same tangled wig that would break any brush that runs through it. Every day, same pair of shoes. She has worn her brown koi-koi shoes so much that if she took them off, they would walk to her house by rote. Always bragging about her savings culture and how she pays school fees for her sibling and rent for her mother as if we are the irresponsible ones. To even buy lunch at the canteen is a war for her. Nibbling on biscuits like a nursery school child. It beats me how a young woman would refuse to take care of herself and then give her money to a man. Things women do for love are mind-blowing.

P.S.: Please everyone, delete this chat. HR isn't supposed to be spreading gist.

TO: PastorTitusMinistries
FROM: Njideka1997
SUBJECT: About Odogwu
2ND DECEMBER

Pastor,

Greetings in the name of the Lord. I hope everything is going well. Thank you for the prayer pamphlet you gave me last month. I have been using it for my morning devotions and my understanding of the role of the Holy Spirit in my life has changed. Even my neighbors whom you gave copies to say they've never read the word of God explained so lucidly. You're a gift to the body of Christ. I'm glad you're my spiritual father. I was in your office earlier today to report a private matter but I learned you went to Abeokuta for the Fire on My Mountain Retreat. I am certain you will surely return with even more fire for the Lord.

Pastor, I know you are big on us believers loving our neighbors as we love ourselves and blessing them when they trespass against us. Yet there are times I want the ground to swallow those who have brought me harm like it did Dathan and Abiram in the days of Moses. I want lightning from heaven to strike them blind as it did Saul en route to Damascus.

You have also told us that our enemies aren't flesh and blood, but spirits. But this enemy of mine is a person: Brother Odogwu. We've been dating for nine months and he asked me to lend him some money, N700K to be precise. He needed the rest of the money to complete payment for a car, if not, he could lose a good deal. I thought to myself: If we were going to get married, as he said, then I needed to support him in buying this car. A man with an automobile has an easier time negotiating with the in-laws; that way they're convinced if worse comes to worst, their daughter wouldn't walk under the sun like some aimless peasant. I gave him the money. In hindsight, I know I should have asked why he didn't borrow from his guys or family members. But I'm a supportive girlfriend. And a supportive girlfriend, just like a supportive wife, is a helpmeet. My man's car is as good as mine. After all, he'd encouraged me to start saving. He'd frown when I came home with a new dress from Miss Kay's boutique and tell me that earning and spending never made one a billionaire. I thought to myself, This guy has sense. This guy is a keeper.

But here's where the story gets sad: I haven't seen Odogwu or heard from him in weeks. I went to his house in Jakande and found it padlocked. His neighbors said he moved. Moved to where? I asked. They looked at me and shook their heads. I was not the only girl who came to look for him. Rumor has it that he left the country with a lot of women's money.

I write to you for spiritual help and counsel, and also to check if he left you any money for me. I am desperate and I don't know how I'll face my ailing mother this Christmas with no gifts to offer. I had planned to take her for a CT scan for her cough. Over the phone, she tries to stifle it but I can hear her chest wheezing. I can hear my mother dying slowly.

Help me, please.

TO: Njideka1997
FROM: PastorTitusMinistries
SUBJECT: I don't blame you
3RD DECEMBER

Njideka, my daughter,

In my line of holy duty, I encounter people like you who, without haste, make us, preachers, accomplices in the crimes of our members. When I heard you came to the office, I was excited and looked forward to your note—and to think that I anticipated good news. I've been interceding for all my members, praying they experience miraculous breakthroughs in all areas of their lives. Let the barren rock her babies in her arms, let the jobless find gainful employment, let the divorced woman obtain favor again in the eyes of her estranged husband. If I don't pray for my flock, who will? This is what I have pledged my whole life to.

But I read your note and I refrain from responding to you in the manner you deserve. I'll show restraint and treat you like the lost and prodigal sheep you are.

First of all, you've been dating Odogwu for nine months. Enough time to bring a baby into this world, and you didn't think it wise to obtain my blessings before constituting a relationship with a member of *my* congregation? You preferred running around town with him, eschewing spiritual counsel and the principles of Christian courtship. Now your evil works have imploded in your face, and you hurry to me? If you find my tone harsh, I refuse to apologize. It's my duty as your spiritual father to reprove you in love. I've told you young girls: dating is a worldly concept introduced wrongly to the body of Christ through the vapid culture of Hollywood and Nollywood. This hopping from person to person will deplete your value such that when you finally find your God-approved husband, the man who should be a covering over your head, you become as washed up and rinsed out as old fabric. I've warned severally: preserve yourself from these shameful outcomes. If you gave your so-called boyfriend 700K, then I'm certain you must have given him your body and allowed him to defile you.

Secondly, you had such a huge amount of money in your coffers, and you watched me grovel every Sunday for funds to fix the church roof. You were there that Sunday three months ago when the rain came suddenly and almost blew away the little covering we had over our heads. The dignitaries who visited our parish for the Onyia's child dedication left grumbling and drenched. Everybody expected me to command the deluge to cease as if I were a mere juju rainmaker. You, Njideka, watched the church membership drop during the rainy season because parents complained their children caught a cold in the house of the Lord. Yet you sat tightly on your purse while the church fell into ridicule. Rather than help, you put your money in a bag of holes. How many times will I teach you that man is fickle and only God deserves our trust?

Lastly, if you're insinuating Odogwu gave me a tithe of this said money, remember that every offering goes straight to God and I'm merely a vessel, a conduit that channels these gifts to heaven.

As you asked, Abeokuta is glorious. There are many ministers here who have come to withdraw from the cares of this world and seek the face of the Lord. I'm not supposed to mingle with civilian affairs as I undertake this spiritual journey. Refrain from writing to me until I return to Lagos. When you're willing, come around so I can pray for the restoration of your soul.

TO: Njideka1997
FROM: chimeenwankwo
SUBJECT: Mama is sick
6TH DECEMBER

Sister Njide,

How is work? I hope you're doing well. I passed my common entrance with a distinction, and I scored 450 over 500 in the Unity School examination. Mama was so happy she cooked jollof rice for me and killed a chicken. She asked me to choose any part of it I liked, and I picked the bum because it's juicy. I was happy to see Mama happy and she said I will do well in life just like my big sister, Njideka. And thank you for that rechargeable lantern. It helped me study at night whenever NEPA took the light.

Sister, Mama has started coughing blood again. She tried to hide it and said that the dust from the building construction in the market was getting to her. But I caught her washing her bloodied handkerchief and shaking her head the way she did those days before Papa died. Sister, it is bad. The cough syrup in Okwudili's chemist doesn't work. Mama no longer pours the content into a measuring spoon. She drinks straight from the bottle and falls asleep afterwards. Customers come into the shop and when they see her dozing, they hiss and head to the next shop. Items disappear every day because Mama cannot keep her eyes open to catch the thieves. I want to ask her but I am afraid she will scold me, but I am sure she is sick. Can you call her and bully her to go to the hospital? She listens to you. Also, can you send her money? Her shop is struggling and the little wares left are collecting dust.

Tochi's brother in the city bought him a bicycle and whenever I beg him, he doesn't let me ride. I sometimes steal it when he leaves it leaning on the wall and I ride a little before he reappears. One day, Mama saw me sneaking away with the bicycle and she pulled my ear so hard I feared she'd tear it off, telling me to be content with what I had. Please, Sister Njide, will you buy me my own bicycle, bigger and more beautiful than Tochi's? I want it in color blue. Blue is now my favorite color. No longer red.

TO: odogwu.felix
FROM: Njideka1997
SUBJECT: Odogwu, my mother is sick
6TH DECEMBER

Odogwu,
    If I have done you wrong and your disappearance is your way of punishing me, then I apologize. I am appealing to your good conscience as a man whose mother is also dear to him. Put me in your shoes. My mother is sick. How do I explain to people that after all these years of working, I am unable to foot her medical bills? How do you expect me to sit back and watch sickness ravage my poor mother's body? I want her alive to benefit from all the sacrifices she made for me. Odogwu, I appeal to that side of you that is a doting son, that side of you that is restless at the news of your mother's inconvenience, have mercy on me and return my money.

TO: Adanma.nwosu
FROM: Njideka1997
SUBJECT: I am ready for the police case
11TH DECEMBER

Ada,
    I am ready. Chimee told me my mother's health is declining and I have no means to take her to the hospital. You can tell your zaddy about me. I'm done being soft. Odogwu has exhausted the grace period. I don't care if his mother gets hurt. It's all on her and her evil son.

TO: Mustapha.Dauda
FROM: Adanma.nwosu
SUBJECT: Arrest a fraudster's mom
11TH DECEMBER

Sexy Zaddy,

    How are you coping with this new station? Is your wife still cooking watery soup and starving your stomach and your you-know-what? Do you miss me? Shhh! Don't answer. Remember what happened the last time you got emotional? A senior police officer of the Federal Republic of Nigeria shouldn't be found in that posture. The last time we spoke, you complained that your new station was in a village, too interior and underdeveloped, and all you do each day is settle petty quarrels between villagers. A missing chicken. A poisoned dog. Farmland disputes. Did you find the chief's missing bicycle that caused such an uproar the last time I visited? Are the herdsmen still letting their cattle eat the villagers' crops? I know you are a man committed to serving his country, and I'm still not over the fact that the wicked men in power deliberately removed you from Lagos and sent you to the backwaters, only to install their people in your stead.

    Remember that night at Freedom Park where you held me on your lap and you swore by your lapels and baton to do anything for me? That night the live band played highlife music from the 1980s and you held me, unafraid that your wife's friends might send her pictures of us together. If you still love me, I want you to do something for me. My best friend got swindled by a man who promised her marriage and he has reportedly fled the country. His mother, however, lives in your jurisdiction and I believe she is an accomplice. Her name is Mrs. Carol Ejindu Odogwu. She runs a vegetable store at the village market. She is quite old but agile. I believe she would know a thing or two about her son's whereabouts. If you need to speak with my friend, I can supply you with her contact details. Just don't ask her out, okay? You are mine.

    Kisses.

THE NIGERIAN POLICE
STATEMENT OF ACCUSED PERSON
NAME: Mrs. Carol Odogwu
NATIONALITY/TRIBE: Nigeria/Igbo

AGE: 59yrs
OCCUPATION: Market woman
RELIGION: Christianity
ADDRESS: The Round-about after Igwe's compound
(Written with the help of an interpreter.)

I am Mrs. Carol Odogwu, a native of Ubakala, Umuahia South Local Government. I am a petty trader. I sell ugu leaves that I grow in my backyard. I also sell yellow peppers, bitter leaf, and okra. I have, from my hard work, raised two exceptional sons: Felix and Mattias. I don't look for anyone's trouble, ask the other market women. Even when they gossip about me and spread all kinds of lies about my children, accusing them of unclean wealth, I keep my face straight and beckon my customers. If my progress is paining them, let it pain them. The formula is simple: My boys work hard and that's why they can roof my house and buy me a newer bicycle, cleaner than the Igwe's. I don't need to sell these vegetables. My sons sustain me. I suffered to raise them while their father squandered his pension in beer parlors. I only come to the market to quell boredom. My sons' successes have made me an easy target for envy and jealousy. It is not my fault that God has blessed the works of their hands. Mattias is a banker in Abuja and Felix is an astute businessman who has a gift for buying and selling, just like his mother. What does he sell? Things, that's all I know. The boy sells things.

But why would anyone begrudge my good fortune? Am I God? Just yesterday, someone stole two chickens from my compound. When I confronted Mama Rebecca, she raised a sandstorm and told me that it was my sons who were thieves, not her. Mama Rebecca has been a mighty thorn in my flesh ever since my husband hastily married her to spite me because I refused to sponsor his drunkard ways. He is dead now. Good riddance. But he left me this other woman to contend with daily.

This afternoon, as I was minding my business in my tiny stall, making slow but steady sales, two police officers came to me and asked about my last son, Felix. They didn't greet me, arrogant young boys. My sons can pay their salaries comfortably without breaking a sweat. Just because they are dressed in uniforms does not mean they should forget to respect an elderly woman. Of course, I refuse to tell them where my son is. If you were a mother, would you tell? These days, crazy things are happening. Anyone can pretend to be a police officer to press sensitive information from you. So I asked them, Why do you want to know my son's whereabouts? Why are you looking for my trouble this hot afternoon? Don't you have something better to do? Suddenly they produced a piece of paper and said that I must follow them to the police station. At that point, all those gossipy market women abandoned their wares and looked at me intently, some giggling, some nodding their heads in assent to my disgrace. I thought this was what the young people call April Fool, but when the policemen wouldn't budge and even spoke to me more roughly, I followed them. It was Mama Nkasi, the only person that I trust, who promised to pack up my wares.

Now I am told my son, Felix, defrauded a certain Njideka Nwankwo of the sum of N700,000. How? My child a fraudster? Tufiakwa! My only problem in this life is that I underestimate my enemies. How can Mama Rebecca do this to me? Why has she connived with my enemies to bring me shame and disgrace? I swear to the Creator who made me, if my son is a thief, may I run raving mad, butt naked on the streets. If my son is a criminal, may lightning strike me down this very second. May I not live to see the next day. No, don't tell me to calm down. Who are you to tell me to calm down?

TO: Mustapha.Dauda
FROM: Sergeant Ikon
SUBJECT: Woman in our custody faints
13TH DECEMBER

Good evening, Sir,

I apologize for writing you so late. I know you have warned us not to disturb you after 7:00 P.M. I have called your number but it is switched off. The woman in our custody slumped and began foaming in the mouth. We have poured water on her and shaken her vigorously but she is unresponsive. The clinic is closed—the nurses are still on strike because their salaries have not been paid for months—and the nearest hospital is thirty minutes away. There is no fuel in any of the trucks. What do we do? If we take her to the hospital, who will pay the bill? We are scrolling through her phone to see if there are any relatives of hers we can get in touch with before things get out of hand. Please tell us what to do before she dies in our hands.

TO: Mustapha.Dauda
FROM: Mattias Odogwu
SUBJECT: Woman in your custody is my mother
14TH DECEMBER

Dear Sir,

 When I received a call that my mother was in a critical state, I did not know what to make of the news. I thought she was skipping her meds and being stubborn as usual. It surprised me to learn she was arrested and refused the right to call a lawyer or any of her relatives. I do not write to make trouble, even though my mother was not accorded her right as a true citizen of this country. I understand that right now in her sickbed, she remains under your custody. Officer, we both know what this entails. If I follow due process, that is, hire a lawyer and wait in line to get a court hearing, my mother will not survive this ordeal. Yes, Felix is the one you want, but he is no longer in the country. Would you hold an old woman to ransom till an errant son returns?

 My brother has the fond habit of dragging the family name in the mud and this time, he has dragged my mother's health into his filthiness. I know Njideka, and I am aware she gave my brother this money. It is unfortunate things have turned this way. Right now, what my family and I can produce is half a million naira. When my brother returns, he can handle the rest of the payment.

 Please accept the deal, Officer, so that I can take my mother home and tend to her health.

TO: Adanma.nwosu
FROM: Mustapha.Dauda
SUBJECT: When are you coming to see Zaddy
16TH DECEMBER

My Tomato Jos.
 My reggae and blues.
 My gin and lime.
 When are you coming to revive my youth? Baby, you abandoned me in this village for mosquitoes to suck away my virility. That's unfair. I have not heard from you in two months and the one time you write me, you send me on

a suicide mission. That old woman almost died in my hands but her son bailed her. I was able to retrieve N350,000 from him and I have sent it to your friend. N350,000 is not such a bad deal. She is a lucky girl. So many people never recover their money. Once it enters the hands of these swindlers, it is gone! I hope you are not like her, these city girls that fleece us old men to squander on young men. If I hear that you have a small boyfriend eh, I will arrest him and all his family members. That's my love language: arrest.

I just credited your account with N50,000. That's your flight money. You warned me the other time that you do not travel by road. I hear you, Queen Bathsheba. Come by air my beautiful one, come and make me a man again. These chicken and dog cases are emasculating me.

TO: Adanma.nwosu
FROM: Njideka1997
SUBJECT: Thank you
21ST DECEMBER

Ada,

Umuahia is as quiet as ever. I arrived two nights ago and it feels good to be home again. Mama and Chimee have filled my ears with stories of their escapades and we laugh far into the night. No, I did not tell Mama what happened. I just told her that the young man I was seeing in the city is not who he said he was. She sighed and held my hands. "Your person will find you."

Can you believe it? I saw him in my dream last night. I was in my house in Lagos, and he knocked on my door and I let him in. I hugged him. So tight. I was afraid to ask what happened; why did the calls go unreturned? Why did the text, the chats, the emails go unanswered? I pretended not to be angry. Then he fried me an omelet for breakfast. Even in my dream, his cooking was still the bomb, my favorite thing about him. After I showered, he picked out an outfit for me. He dressed me hurriedly and when the clock said 7:30 a.m., I told him I had to hurry to work. But he held me at the door and kissed me for long, he said this would keep him in my thoughts. I managed to wriggle out of his arms, laughing so contentedly as I ran to work.

Then I woke up. What a rubbish dream. I blame it on the heat. Umuahia still suffers terrible power outages. The last rain came, redolent with dust, ushering in Harmattan. We received it with the resignation of a farewell full of sighs. We hoped it would ease the air of restlessness, the heat that kept us up at night, that made us sleep without clothes on, fanning the air with old newspapers, twirling in our nightdresses, sodden with sweat. I tried to sleep again, to see if he'd return to me so that I could skin him alive. But sleep did not return, and neither did Odogwu.

I went Christmas shopping with Chimee and bought him a bicycle, and I also sent my mother to the hospital. We are awaiting the result. The doctor says it looks bad. My heart breaks each time I have to pull out my wallet and spend money, but what do I do? I cheer myself up with the fact that some of the money I lost was retrieved. Half bread is still a miracle. Mama must not know that I am struggling. She already has a lot to worry about.

Ada, I don't know what I would do without you. Thank you for everything. My December salary was deducted but I won't complain. Such is life. I should have listened to you when you told me the guy was a fraud. I was convinced he had changed when he started showing up, ordering me lunch that was delivered to my office because I told him I didn't like the food at the canteen. His texting even improved. My phone would chime at exactly six in the morning and I'd wake to another declaration of his unyielding affection. He said his happiness lived here, with me, his joy resided in my arms.

Will I ever love anyone again, Ada? The motions, the niceties of new romance are for those who can muster the energy. I have lost strength. No one knew me like he did. My favorite ugba joint, the way I like my noodles cooked, the way I want my back massaged after work, the right spot to knead. I am not ready to prim my manners afresh, to preen before someone new. I fell for him hoping this would be the last and I'd finally hang my boots and ease into home. I did not need to be anything else but myself around him. I thought he was home.

PORTRAITS OF MY AUNT ON HER SICKBED
YEE HENG YEH

1. Sick people usually look sick
   but the fact was my aunt
   was positively glowing. They said it started
   on the first night, when they removed the clog
   from her vessel and her relieved blood
   ran so light and quick under her paper-lantern skin
   that she began to flicker with this fire of life—
   first like the quiet ember at a joss stick's tip,
   the sapphire of the gas stove flame,
   then brighter, bolder, until she was blinding white,
   like the noon sun cut out in the shape of an aunt
   and tucked in a hospital bed.

   They had to hang black sheets
   as thick as dictionaries around her bed
   so the other patients could sleep.
   Anyone visiting would have to wear
   those glasses you put on to look at a solar eclipse.
   And there was no way to take a photo with her
   because all that came out was a pure, blank square,
   as if nothing and no one was ever there,
   so we got in a painter and people would pose
   while he captured—through resourceful use
   of lines and shapes and colors—
   what the lens of the camera couldn't.
   His wisdom was in understanding
   that beauty was never where you seek it;
   the trick was to look, really look,
   from the corner of your eye.

2. The worst part was that the stroke
took from my aunt even her words.
It was as if the strings in her throat
had been cut loose and her voice
now dangled like a broken chime in the wind.
All that we heard was her larynx knocking
against itself like it was both the visitor
and the door of the person who wasn't home.

So imagine our surprise
when she started speaking again.
At first we cheated and mimicked
the shape of her lips, the gestures
of her tongue, filling in the blanks
ourselves. But soon it was there:

a whisper, but there.
Air gathered itself the way a storm
builds its own courage until—

a word. It bounced off
her chin and came to rest
on the blanket as we huddled around,
lost for words ourselves.
Then one of us cradled it in the cushion
of a palm and gingerly slipped it
into a glass jar.

In this way we hoarded the stray words
that her cords duly dropped off
like a fruit basket each morning:
as the saying goes, each one
was as treasured as gold.
When we finally had enough
to string together a sentence

her new voice had already ripened,
full and heavy as a melon.
We had no more use for the jar of words
so we forgot about

it except for the times in the future
when who we were now would be just a memory
and we would lift the lid to hear again
those first few rattling seeds of sound,
the beginnings of my aunt's new voice,

so different from that old one
now that she was unlike the rest of us
who did not once know
what it really meant to be silenced.

3. It's true, my cousin told my mom,
she saw you everywhere
in the hospital. My mom
had not made the trip to visit my aunt
during Chinese New Year,
which was when my aunt
had her stroke. She must have missed
you so much, my cousin said.

How else could they explain it:
My mom sweeping the floor in the ward.
Sitting by the bed, studying her Korean and German.
Dancing by the evening window.
Bent over the sewing machine
that had materialised the minute she did…

Unbeknownst to herself my mom
had been living two lives, her quantum twin
standing in for her six hundred kilometers away.

Time had slipped up and for a moment
allowed this entity, stitched with the thread
of memory, to do what she had to do.

I thought then about dreams, about love,
how we could save each other
by not being there. Well I'm here now,
said my mom, you don't need that ghost
anymore. And look, I made you this—
now she held up a loose dark-olive gown
that spilled from her fingers like a flag
of feathers. Do you like it?

She usually likes bright colors, said my cousin.
Do you like it? my mom asked again, laughing.
It'll do, my aunt said softly. Nothing else.

4. Enough
of fiction and its diminutions.
This is the truth:
The way that we talked about her
in the third person as my aunt lay there.
The way that she did not smile, not with her eyes.
The way that I dared not touch her
(I had never touched her before this).
The way that they kept telling her
not to worry, her grown-up kids are all right.
The fact that life went on in a single room,
the TV a window to the faces of this world,
the real window a thing of beauty
with no words, no faces.

Also the way a poem eases a memory out of you.
Makes remembering possible by excising the pain.

The finished poem steps over its own writing
and becomes—almost—joy.

The poem remains silent about the myeloma,
the cheating husband, the body's intolerances,
but even so this is the truth,
and the rest, too, all of it.
You must know: none of this is enough.
Here we've only just begun.

FICTION
THE COVE
CJ GREEN

I found my grandfather at the edge of the dock. He was staring into the water, crouching knees to chest, the way a child would when inspecting a bug or some other such treasure. It struck me as the kind of position he should have progressed beyond, but something about his ligaments made it more comfortable for him to assume childlike poses—he liked sitting cross-legged or, on his sofa, curling into a ball. My mother encouraged him to try yoga, and whenever she did, he would pretend as if he were hearing of it for the first time. I think he preferred to keep busy with things he discovered himself; he liked being the only one who knew about a thing. Beyond that, no one could understand his interest in oysters, why he started growing them off his little dock on Long Cove. He liked the taste of a grilled oyster all right but gave away more than he ate, handing off bushel baskets to neighbors and childhood friends.

It was September, and the youngest oysters were small, no bigger than a thumbnail. They rested one on top of another, not unlike barnacles in the nearest cage. All together there must have been a thousand. My grandfather would wait another two years to harvest them, and in that time they would quadruple in size just by sitting there.

Standing nearby, my sister Lindsey pointed out that humans grow faster than that, and brandished her daughter Reagan as evidence. In two years, Reagan had gone from the size of a bean in her womb to a small person now determined to fling herself into the river while Lindsey made a show of physically restraining her, saying, "Come on, stop that, get away from there, come on, let's go, don't do that, get away from there." To Reagan, Lindsey's voice was clearly white noise. It crossed my mind that Lindsey might be too preoccupied with her daughter, to the point where she was willing to put down oysters to exalt her, but still, I took her point: there was something unsurprising about the oysters, the way they accreted over the course of seasons, gaining mass as algae and star grass and sediment washed over them with the tides.

"Look!" Reagan shrieked, and it sounded like, *Luke!* She was pointing toward an oyster cage, which my grandfather had begun hauling out from the river. White water spilled out from between its chain links and crashed down like a waterfall. My grandfather shook the cage up and down to empty it of sediment, before hoisting the whole thing up onto the dock so Reagan could inspect it. "What's that? What's that? What's that?"

"It's an oyster, it's a shell, it's seaweed, it's a stick. Let's go, get away from there, come on." Taking Reagan's hand, Lindsey turned and noticed me standing there. "Oh, perfect, you made it," she said. Her eyes, meeting mine, conveyed something like relief. Stepping toward me for a hug, she explained that she'd recently given up caffeine.

Lindsey was always giving up something. Smoking, gluten, now caffeine. I anticipated a day soon when she would renounce alcohol, profess herself an alcoholic, because, after all, she was. We all had our dependencies—my father to nicotine, my mother to control. My grandmother, Nan, was harder to classify, but I imagined religious fervor was her drug of choice. Like all of us, she had been raised Catholic but in her forties converted to Evangelicalism before adopting, in her sixties, Buddhism. According to my mother, Nan meditated at least an hour a day. Before sunrise she would sit in a lawn chair facing the river, her gaze so indistinct no one dared to disturb her. I figured it was her intention to detach from whatever challenge my grandfather was presenting. He was the vine from whose branches all of our sins seemed to flow. When my mother was a child, he'd lost all of their family savings at casinos in Colonial Beach. I was young when I learned that—he told me and Lindsey directly, with a tone of confession. The casinos had been strategically located at the end of long piers, which stretched far enough over the river to be licensed in Maryland, where gambling was legal. In middle-age he replaced gambling with less expensive habits. I watched him trying new things: small game hunting, crabbing, oyster gardening. Having some kind of return—the possibility of winning—was crucial.

He once explained that mature oysters could filter up to fifty gallons of water every day, and for the same reason were almost solely responsible for keeping the bay and all its tributaries clean. At the time, he had been standing at his grill holding a pair of silver tongs, waiting for his latest harvest to pop open from the heat, while I'd stood nearby, shucking their hot shells. I had asked whether we should really be eating filterers of filthy water, to which he'd barely made the effort to shrug, uninterested in any concern at all.

While Reagan poked her fingers through the oyster cage, I pointed to it and asked, "Anything ready to eat?"

My grandfather shook his head, said nothing. I looked at Lindsey as if to say, *I tried.*

Their rambler was a short walk off the bank. With Lindsey and Reagan, I went back up along the footpath of moss and sandy dirt and found our mother, with Nan and Aunt Kari. They had come outside to sit in the shade of a wide magnolia.

"Hi," I told everyone, "hi."

"Hi, hi, hi," Reagan repeated, twisting out of Lindsey's grip and flinging herself at my mother.

"You didn't have to come," Nan said, standing to give me a hug. She was convinced all family visits were an inconvenience.

Nan had taken to wearing a swimsuit at all times of day. Sometimes it was accompanied by sweatpants or a visor. For now, it was just the polka dots—yellow, pink—and her thin legs, browned by summer sun.

I took a seat beside my mother, who asked about my job at the restaurant, my apartment, my paintings. We chatted a bit before Lindsey nudged me and asked, "So what's your strategy?"

"What do you mean?" I asked, knowing what she meant.

"Your strategy," she repeated. "About him. You'll get him to talk how?"

"He can do what he wants," I said. "I don't care."

I guess my only strategy was not to have one: I intended to ignore the fact of our grandfather's silence, in hopes of making it seem boring and not worth keeping up. If I failed, I couldn't be perceived to have tried.

"That's right," Nan said, shaking her head sadly but also in acceptance. "He can do what he wants."

It was my private suspicion that my grandfather's silence was a performance, an art piece of sorts. He wasn't a stranger to wanting attention. My grandfather liked simple things—a quiet house on the river, a long, monogamous marriage—but he also liked a show. A little surprise. On their fiftieth anniversary, he had convinced Nan to get a tattoo. They'd arrived at their party with TRUE LOVE FOREVER inked over their knuckles.

At first, Nan had thought he was having some kind of stroke, that part of his brain had begun to deteriorate. It pained me to imagine. He was willing to nod, or shake his head, but to anything requiring more than that he would simply act as though he hadn't heard. Aside from this, he was basically normal. Every morning he ate his usual breakfast of eggs—whisked with skim milk, microwaved—and coffee. In the afternoons he would bike a half mile to the town square, and at night he went to sleep without trouble. After a few days, Nan worried he was giving her the silent treatment, that he was angry, that he was sad. She called my aunt, who called her sister, who was my mother, who called my sister. They each drove the distance to my grandparents' house and took a turn trying to crack him. His commitment to silence was attended by a sense of mystery and a feeling that, with a concerted enough effort, someone would be able to solve it.

Aunt Kari went first. As Nan later described it, Kari conducted what amounted to a thorough medical exam. Though she had only completed a year of nursing school, she was often relied upon in our family as a medical professional. She asked if he could hear what she was saying, and he nodded. She stuck a line of masking tape down the hallway and asked him to walk along it. She asked him to stick out his tongue, shined a flashlight down his throat, asked if he was in any pain, and he shook his head. "Looks normal," she declared then, almost in disappointment, slumping, but by then Nan seemed calmer, as if she had caught on to something. "He'll talk," she said with a sigh, "when he's ready."

My mother refused to accept this. She went in for high drama. She arrived with a bang, flying in through the front door, throwing down her bags, demanding some answers. "What the hell is going on? Is this some kind of joke?" To this, my grandfather stood and gave my mother a long hug, from which she broke free. Crying, she begged him to please say even just one word. Why wasn't he acting like himself? Nan's attempts to settle her only upset her further. By the time she gave up, she had accumulated a small monument of crumpled Kleenex.

Reportedly, my sister took a lower-key approach. Lindsey arrived with a bottle of El Dorado, spun the cap off it, poured two glasses, offered him one and, sitting side-by-side on the dock behind the house, they drank. Around them the sunlight faded. I knew exactly what those sunsets were like. I had seen them many times over the years, bright pink over the river, the calm that falls over the water as if it were settling in for the evening, becoming as smooth and still as glass, the subtlest ripple of the surface like the chest of someone sleeping in peace. Lindsey had been determined to not say anything. It was her intention to wait him out. He could be stubborn, but she was his granddaughter, and stubbornness was in her genes. She had assumed he felt a certain softness toward her and might confide in her the way he hadn't with anyone else. They had each drunk two glasses in silence before her frustration came out. When she poured herself a third, he gave her a meaningful look. His eyes were big and dark, almost the color of the river, but only once you're submerged five feet under the surface of it. It was a gentle look he gave her, a smile without a smile, then he too poured his third glass.

No one expected me to make any progress with him. Between my grandfather and me, there was no special connection. There was no special disconnection, either, except the natural kind resulting from distances of age and geography. Now that he wasn't talking, we had more in common than ever. For my whole life relatives had observed that I didn't say much. "He's shy," my mother would always explain on my behalf. I figured my quiet seemed like stupidity, and in some way it probably was. I had many thoughts, but they struggled to find their way out. I might have imagined that as his only male descendant I would have a particular kind of influence, but he always preferred Lindsey to me, and if she had failed, then I figured so would I.

I went anyway. The drive took about three hours. Before setting off, I checked my phone, and a black cloud passed over the sky of my weather app. It looked like a glitch, but maybe smoke, maybe an omen of a dark thing coming. The actual sky looked fine: blue, as usual, with wispy white clouds, though fires had been burning in California, three thousand miles away. I recalled that last summer the fires had gotten so bad that smoke journeyed from that end of the continent to this one, obscuring the eastern horizon, scratching my throat.

I intended to stay one night, on the couch. I dropped my bag beside it. The house smelled of salt and wet dog. The couch was covered in dog fur, remnants of Lucy, my grandparents' mutt, an untrainable nightmare for whom they had expressed uncomplicated love, who had died two months prior. I wondered if my grandfather's silence wasn't an expression of grief. He had buried Lucy at the foot of a nearby wax myrtle. "No more dogs," he'd vowed after that, and I wondered if he was grieving not only Lucy but all the dogs he resolved not to love.

He hadn't always lived by the river. With two young daughters, he and Nan had moved around Richmond, spiraling farther out of the city, from townhouse to apartment as rent escalated, but there seemed to be some boomerang effect for many people his age, that if you grew up near the water, you were fated to return to it, and that's what he did. He never owned property until a decade ago when, without preamble, he bought the rambler five miles from the neighborhood he'd been raised in. It had been vacant since the nineties. It was a white one-story house in a quiet neighborhood—more a road than a neighborhood—alongside the river. Mostly retirees lived there, or people who only came on weekends.

The last time I came was with Tala, in June. We'd been together about three months by then. She kept calling my grandparents' house a "lake house," and I feared she would be disappointed when she saw it. It was her first and only time there, a hot weekend—too humid to spend much time outside, except for short dips in the water—so we passed two days in the sun room. Wryly Tala asked if there were any baby pictures to be seen, and Nan smiled. She kept her photos in loose collections of folders and shoeboxes secured with rubber bands. Flipping through, we saw me and my sister at Reagan's age, in sandboxes, gnawing the mouths of empty beer bottles. We saw cousins of cousins, kids I'd never seen before, with their feet dug into the mud off the river bank. "You don't know them?" Tala asked, and I shook my head.

"Oh, there's Reggie," Nan said, pointing to a young man in army fatigues, my grandfather's brother.

"Who's that?" Tala asked, curious.

"Reggie," my mother repeated, then gave a deep nod to convey some secret knowledge was passing between herself and Nan, "before."

"Before what?" I asked, realizing I'd never learned how he died.

Through a big grimace, my mother explained that he'd been shot to death—"a holdup, a freak thing," as she put it. Next to me, Tala listened in silence, twisting her black hair absently around her finger. "He was twenty-three," my mother concluded, before returning the photo to the shoebox and selecting another.

I could have pressed for more information, but Nan had already put another photo in front of me. It was of her and my grandfather. "This one," she said. "This is the one. You look just like him, don't you think?" The photo had been taken before they were married, but not long before. I saw myself in it, in him. "In the eyes," Nan said, leaning back to study mine. Though sepia, it was obvious his face was flushed, from either the sun or happiness generally, and he stood beside Nan, who looked like a little girl hoisting up an enormous striped bass as long as her legs. Nan seemed to have no attachment to the photo, so she gave it to me. She had reached a point in life where she was constantly trying to get rid of things. I took it home, lost it.

"Your family does this weird thing," Tala noted after that. "They're very withholding." She was still wearing her black bikini beneath a pair of paint-splattered overalls. We had just gotten back to the studio apartment—both a studio, where we painted, and an apartment, where I lived, where Tala sometimes spent the night. In a corner, she had staked a canvas she was working on and, spread over an old bedsheet, some palettes and brushes. Opposite hers, I kept mine. She took a seat up on the linoleum countertop, tied up her hair, and said, "It's like they care too much about what you think to tell you who they really are."

I considered this. My family did have a tendency to let slip some new information about their lives or histories, almost incidentally, right when I was beginning to think I knew all there was to know. Last year my mother revealed that Aunt Kari's husband Mike had had another kid—I had a secret half cousin. When I asked why she never mentioned this, my mother asked why she ever would have; Mike's secret offspring didn't have any technical relation to me. And after Tala dumped me, my father tried to console me by explaining that when he was my age, he, also, had been dumped. For the first time, I understood that my mother wasn't the only woman he'd loved. I shouldn't have been surprised, but no one had ever mentioned Barbara before. My father revealed that their breakup hadn't been easy. It hadn't *not* been a blowup. He said it felt big at the time but then again, so did everything, when it came to your first love.

As that morning progressed into afternoon, we congregated in the backyard and soon began to talk about him as though he weren't there. Sitting in a circle, we performed, effectively, his eulogy.

My mother, with typical drama, recalled how verbose he had been—God, the stories he would tell! You couldn't get him to shut up. At that, I stole a glance at him, and he seemed to be smiling at the memory, as if he too were bidding a private farewell to the person he had been.

Aunt Kari commemorated the love she'd witnessed between him and Nan, what she called self-sacrificial commitment. Clearly touched, he took Nan's hand, displaying the letters on their knuckles, still fresh with ink, almost aggressively bold, velvet black.

Lindsey said she'd never heard the story of their meeting, and my mother assured her, "This is a good one."

Nan crossed her legs in preparation of the telling. She said they met during Vietnam. She'd been an administrator at Fort Benning, and he the worst recruit the United States had ever drafted. From the moment he touched down at basic training he hadn't spoken a word that wasn't in French. Instead of "Sir! Yes, sir!" he shouted, "Oui, monsieur! Oui!" His level of French was that of someone who'd taken three years in high school, thus what he was able to express was limited. A drill sergeant blackened his eye before he was detained in the on-base stockade and slapped with an Other Than Honorable Discharge. Nan was assigned to handle his paperwork and came to meet him on his first afternoon in the jail, where she fell under the impression that he was a Frenchman mistakenly conscripted into the U.S. Army. They shared what she called "a sweet kiss" and, imagining that if she were successful he might take her back with him to Paris, or Nice, or wherever in France he was from, she became determined to bring him justice. Eventually she hassled her supervisor with enough passion that an investigation was conducted which turned back that, no, he was not a Parisian but rather an utter moron. "By then I already knew," she concluded, "that he was my moron."

My sister laughed, but I only smiled. Now that my grandfather was no longer telling his stories, they seemed to be growing on their own, becoming more incredible in his silence. Around us, the air was humid and still. In the front yards stood dogwoods, magnolias, poplars, their yellowing leaves so perfectly still they began to look fake.

Later that afternoon, when my grandfather went for his daily bike ride, I decided to follow him. I thought that if I could trail him throughout his day it might tell me something about what was going on in his mind. Once he was at a good distance, pedaling on his old red Schwinn, I took its twin and set off. Were he to look back, I would wave, pretend that I was trying to catch up to him. He never looked back.

He biked at a steady pace. The bikes were for children, I realized, noticing how his knees rose toward the handlebars before noticing the way mine did the same. He was unexpectedly swift, and I felt winded. Spanning ahead the road was flat, faded asphalt, and in it were crushed pebbles and remnants of shells. Dried pine needles collected on the shoulder. He crossed the bridge over the river, up into the town square, where there was a post office, a few old houses, a boarded-up restaurant, a small church, and a gazebo in the middle of the town green. Someone was walking a dog. He raised a hand to whoever it was. A pickup drove past. It was such a quiet place that my grandparents always remarked on the passing cars; they knew whose was whose, and more than two cars during any outing was considered heavy traffic, a bother.

I had thought he would circle the town green and go back. But my grandfather continued past the church and down the road another half mile before turning abruptly left down a lane so narrow and tree covered that I almost missed it. I took the turn more unsteadily than he had and, rounding it, didn't see him. The lane was winding; all the curves were blind. Along it were a few prefab houses, plain but with precisely kept front yards, overshadowed by tall white pines. Eventually the trees gave way to a wall of corn, impassive green stalks on either side of the road. The sun flooded in and strained my eyes. I hooked another blind turn and saw the bike—a flash of red—in a ditch about a hundred feet ahead. It was sideways, its wheels still spinning even as the bike itself was still.

I slowed to a halt. Just beyond the bike, on the far side of the ditch, was my grandfather, crouching exactly as he had been on the dock, knees to chest, at the foot of a small cross—two intersecting wooden bars, painted white—that had been dug into the earth. The cross was unaccompanied by wreaths or bouquets. It was the kind you could drive past a million times without seeing it. From the distance it seemed as if the paint was splintering, maybe molding. It looked old.

For a moment I observed quietly, one foot on a pedal, the other on the road. The high sun gave the place the feeling of a dream. There were no shadows beneath anything. It was peaceful, momentarily, but then full of little itches, gnats buzzing around my head, sweat rolling down my underarms, a mosquito suckling the back of my knee. I stood there until my grandfather dipped forward and touched his forehead to the earth.

I might have audibly exclaimed, let out a sigh of surprise, maybe disgust. I pushed off and rode back to the house where I found my mother in the kitchen. She was slicing a lemon and arranging its little disks in a pan of filleted perch. I asked how my grandfather's brother—her uncle—had died. When the shooting happened.

She was matter-of-fact about it.

"I don't remember," she said.

"How old were you?" I asked.

"Young," she replied airily.

I hadn't expected her to give me any straight answers, so I'd already planned my countermove. "I should talk to him about it," I said.

Uneasily, she swallowed. Surely she wanted her father to talk, about anything, just not about death. It would be easier for everyone, she seemed to think, if she could tell me the story herself.

"I was a kid," she began, setting down the knife. The blade gleamed with juice. "My uncle Reggie was out with your grandfather, at a casino, I think at Colonial Beach." I had been through Colonial Beach a few times and pictured it: empty piers, lone gulls, faded shopfronts where you could imagine people once roved rowdily, generations ago. Like a dried cocoon, something had been inside there once. "At some point," my mother said, "there was a dispute, I mean about money. Your grandfather and Reggie were driving home when another vehicle apprehended them. A man, some thug, had some issue with your grandfather, and Reggie tried to intervene. And he was shot. He didn't die right away. He went to the hospital, was there for a little while before he passed. I remember when Nan told us. She said, 'Something happened.' I remember we visited him in the hospital once. He didn't know we were there, must have been asleep. I remember the shooter was apprehended and no one else got hurt, because of Reggie," she said, "because of what he was willing to do."

I noticed the walls then—how starkly bare they were. No shrines to the dead or to the living. Clean, I could imagine Nan saying, without any frames cluttering them.

"It's hard," my mother said. "I never heard much myself."

Once everyone was asleep, Lindsey and I rifled around the house, in the refrigerator, the cupboards, for anything that wasn't light beer, but my grandparents weren't much of drinkers, and there was no liquor to be found.

I suggested a trip to the ABC store, but only if she paid. I felt liquor wasn't worth what it would cost.

"I can't," she said. "I only have my credit card, and Stan will see." Her husband had begun monitoring her alcohol consumption, I gathered.

We discovered a few Mike's Hards in a cooler in the garage. The cooler seemed to have been forgotten, its lid covered in dust and belly-up ladybugs. The bottles were warm. We figured that, in a spirit of experiment, one of the grandparents had bought them for the other. We grimaced at the first sip. There was something perverse about the warm sweetly bitter lemonade—something enjoyable. It was as if, at our grandparents' house, everything could be different from what it would be anywhere else. We pulled lawn chairs to the front yard, and with a few twigs picked up from the foot of the nearest pine, I started a fire in a fire pit that was just a few stones in a circle of sand. The fire didn't last and was, in minutes, a pile of loosely arranged smoking sticks, but the smoke kept away the mosquitoes until the night fell thoroughly enough that they disappeared on their own. The only life left was ours.

"Any progress?" she asked eventually.

I thought she was asking about our grandfather, but she meant about my life.

"Ha ha," I said.

"I'm serious," she said. "What's new?"

"Nothing," I said. "I'm the same."

She accused me of being my mother's son, to which I said nothing.

"No word?" she pressed. "From Tala?"

"Not since the last time you asked."

I only noticed Lindsey had been tense now that she no longer was. She seemed pleased. Neither Lindsey nor my mother had ever developed any liking toward Tala, and I struggled to understand why.

"You know it's not your fault," Lindsey reminded me.

"I know." But the truth was that it mostly was.

I imagined I could have punched her, pushed her to the ground, and still she would have found a way to care for me. This I took as evidence—not that she loved me, but that I was serving some functional purpose for her. I often wanted to ask her exactly what it was but couldn't get the words out. When she left it was with the stated intention of giving me space to decide how I felt about her, and two months later, I had to admit her plan was working. I missed her. A few days after she left, I called my parents, who called Lindsey, who called me to ask if I wanted to talk about it, but I had nothing to say. It hadn't been a long relationship, but somehow that made it harder to think about, worse to lose. I still lived in the studio, which seemed smaller without the things she'd kept there. In the corner where she used to paint, I had put one of my own canvases. I'd begun layering murky colors, brown, navy, silver. The subject had yet to emerge.

Comparatively, Lindsey's life couldn't have looked better. She was occupied by only new things. In a matter of years she had acquired a boyfriend, a husband, a new house, a baby and, most recently, a newer house, clearly meant to be filled with more babies. I imagined that to own a house like hers required marrying someone like Stan, who was working a job that no one, not even Stan, could really describe. Once, he had mentioned a PowerPoint. Upon meeting him he struck all of us as very nice, with a full, clean beard, good posture, not a single actual fault.

I couldn't get the energy to ask about him and instead asked, "How's the house?" because even an inanimate dwelling somehow seemed more lively than Stan.

"Fine," she said.

"The neighborhood? You like it?"

Lindsey winked into her bottle.

She then told the story of a neighbor with some problem, she wasn't sure what, something of the mind, who lived in an old split-level at the end of her street and whose freezer had become so full of leftover lasagnas that he couldn't close it. The lasagnas had begun to thaw and stink up the whole house, and there had been a neighborhood initiative to help the man bag up all the lasagnas and throw them out.

"Awful," I said.

"No, it was nice," she said. "To see people come together."

"Awful for him, I meant."

"He has neighbors, that's my point," she said. "It's a good neighborhood. We help each other out."

She seemed to be conjuring a set from a TV show. I wondered if that's where she thought she lived. I wondered if that's where I wanted to live.

"Your neighbor doesn't have an aide?" I asked.

"I don't know," she said. "I guess not."

"He needs an aide," I decided, "and a nurse."

"Okay," she said. Then after a moment: "But who will pay for this man's aide and nurse?"

I shrugged. "The government."

"And who will pay the government?"

"The wealthy." I caught her eyes, cracked a smile. "Not me! I'm poor."

We shared a laugh beneath which was the suspicion that I could have been a wealthy taxpayer if only I had chosen to be, and who knows, maybe I could have been. I had done decently enough in college, as in, I had gone, and graduated. Surely I could have done something like Stan. That had always been the expectation, that although I was shy I would one day justify my shyness by revealing that it was the trait of a quiet genius, and "genius," to my family, meant wealth—triple sevens. "You just wait," my grandfather would say. "Mark my words." But I didn't desire money. Of that I was certain. Maybe it was the anxiety of the desire that I didn't desire—the clamorous, constant looking ahead.

For some reason, considering all this made me optimistic. I felt that I was facing up to something, even if I didn't know what. The universe seemed to be expanding right there in the dark. I suggested to Lindsey that we get drunk together more often, and she told me she wasn't drunk. She raised her bottle, and I raised mine.

It was a warm night, so in the front yard, I flipped on the garden hose and filled a blow-up pool our mother had bought for Reagan, a huge pink donut. Bugs, dead and alive, circled in the water as I filled it. With our lemonades, and in full clothes, we joined them, relaxing into the water where we hardly fit at all, our arms and legs dangling out, threatening to destroy the pool's integrity, flatten and deflate it. Because we were no longer children, I wanted to cry, but Lindsey was laughing, and I was crying but laughing to cover it up. Then she was just crying.

I remembered the darkness that had passed over my weather app, the glitch or the omen, and readied myself for whatever was about to emerge through Lindsey's tears.

It was nothing too horrible, and I was relieved. Her daughter wasn't dying of cancer. Stan wasn't cheating on her. She was only overwhelmed, she said.

"I keep thinking of how our time on earth is finite," she said. "Like eighty years on average—we're all very average." How long she had been stewing over life's brevity I could only guess, but I imagined it had something to do with Reagan, whose short burst of life, even for me, called attention to the short burst of everyone's. "If you want something," she went on, "you have to say it. You have to speak up for yourself."

I thought her sermon was beautiful. I told her she was a beautiful person, inside and out, and that I hoped Stan would always recognize this.

"Maybe he just got bored," I said of our grandfather. "Maybe talking bores him now."

She entertained this. "He does get bored of things."

"Maybe it's a spiritual exercise."

"A vow of silence," she ventured.

"That's what I mean," I said.

"Nan doesn't seem too bothered," she said.

"She doesn't," I agreed, then after a minute: "They're weird."

I thought she and Stan were also weird. I thought my parents were weird too, and certainly Kari and her husband Mike, with his secret child, were as well. It made a lot of sense, from that view, that they in turn had found Tala and me weird.

I told Lindsey what I'd seen earlier: our grandfather prostrate over someone's roadside memorial. I said I assumed it was his brother's.

"No," she said. "It's not his brother's. It's his fiancée's, his first fiancée's. You don't know this? He was engaged before Nan."

I closed my eyes.

"He goes there every day," she said.

I leaned back in exhaustion, and confusion, and the pool collapsed under my weight, water sloshing out over me into a puddle in the grass, where I also suddenly was, staring up at the stars which had never appeared to me more like the dust of shattered glass on a roadside. "Everyone knows?" I asked.

"I don't know," she said. "When they moved back here, he started going. I don't know if he planned it, or if it just played out, or what. He's been making these pilgrimages—that's what they're calling them, pilgrimages. I don't know if that's like a joke. I really don't." She went on, "They were high school sweethearts. He proposed, and they were engaged—engagements were shorter back then. They were going to get married. And then she was killed, and he was drafted. Car wreck. That's all I know, that's all."

Instantly I could see them: a blond bob for her, a slim figure beside his, floating in the river, toes peeking through the surface. I wondered where they had left off, what business remained unaddressed, conversations never ended. I wondered when, in the middle of all this, his brother had died. I thought of my grandfather, throwing all of his money into slots. I thought of how, without us doing anything to incite them, horrible things could accrete, one on top of another.

From the backyard came a clatter. We fell completely still—I felt as though I were falling through myself. A shuffle of feet on the back deck, a voice.

With her eyebrows raised, Lindsey mouthed, "What the fuck," as if fearing the worst, maybe an intruder, a burglar. But to me, it just sounded like someone was awake.

Quietly I stood, wet clothes sticking to my skin. She stood, and followed. The air cooled as it moved around us, as we crept over the yard, over the dandelions and plantain weeds.

We edged along the side of the house, peered around the corner, and in the moonlight saw two figures, the hunched forms of our grandparents, disappearing down the path to the dock. They had the posture of burglars in a cartoon, progressing down the footpath on their tiptoes. They were naked, a fact I didn't immediately comprehend, until, in the moonlight, I saw the undeniable plane of my grandfather's back continuing uninterrupted toward the dark slash of a butt crack. Then he, it—the crack—disappeared. There was a splash.

We listened for a minute, but they weren't saying anything. I felt the urge to disappear but lingered another moment. Through the trees we saw ripples of moonlight where they were treading, disturbing the water. I wondered if they were disturbing the oysters nearby, resting on top of each other in their cages. I thought of all the sediment and seaweed that would never stop washing over them. I thought of the shells we shucked every winter, where, inside, their fat hearts were waiting to be scooped out and eaten.

JOURNEY

EROSION
CORY HOWELL HAMADA

It was the spring of last year, after I began walking the Ise Bay down Japan's Pacific coast, that my headaches grew worse. I don't remember when I started to feel unwell, but at some point, when the calm of the bay opened to the ocean, the distance began to give me a sense of vertigo, like I was standing on a cliffside, horizon tilting as I gazed down at whitewash foaming the rocky blue. When I look back, that unsteady feeling mixes with images from the road—flooded rice fields reflecting purple evening, clothes hung to dance on apartment balconies, collapsing houses with leaves peeking through cracked windows, straining for a better view of the outside—and the edges of those memories seem to wear and fray with passing time. Neither can I remember calling Lilly to pick me up. All I can recall of the first few days in the hospital are artificial light streaks and squeaky footsteps drawing near only to pause and fade to silence. My room faced the ruins of a nearby castle, I was told, but I could only see the tops of the cherry blossoms and plum trees that were supposed to burst into color in the spring and stand bare in the winter, and when my eyes would tire from the hours on my phone and I felt the distance flatten between the walls and the bed and the chairs, I'd turn to stare from my window at the orange and yellow leaves breaking off in the wind. At the end of the first week, I began to wonder if the window was just another screen, and crawled along the white tile, tried to pull myself onto a chair to see outside when two nurses rushed in, scolded me, pulled me back to bed and stood looking down at me with laced fingers and concerned looks. As I fell asleep that evening, their low tones drifted from just outside, Hiromi—or maybe it was Manami, I

had trouble telling their voices apart—was expressing concern that maybe the last three dates went poorly because of her, not because of the men, that maybe she was doing something wrong, perhaps she was undesirable? You're not so young anymore, after all. But maybe you should try a different dating app, Tappuru's matches often didn't work well for me either, or if it really gets to that point, why not move to the city for a while? After all, the men are so conservative here.

    I began walking south from Yokkaichi, after an intense stint of work annotating movie director Ozu Yasujiro's high school diary. The morning I set out was pink clouds framing the petrochemical plants that already streamed gray above the docks, lights from the night before still glittering, punctuating the huge orbs of the oil refineries. Yokkaichi is a family trauma, an heirloom nobody can seem to throw away. It's a house that generations have retired in, died in, and continue to haunt with restless spirits, and they all seemed to stir in April 1971 when *The Asahi Shimbun* shocked and outraged the nation by publishing a copy of Fukutomi Isaburo's suicide note. While I understand I must endure suffering for the greater

good, life has grown painful and every breath is agony, he wrote, and I can no longer withstand it. Rather than simply retype the note, the editor reprinted Fukutomi's illegible handwriting—something seen as both overly personal and unduly invasive, even for Japan's most liberal newspaper—and when I saw it for the first time, studying Japan's pollution diseases in a post-war history class, I remember feeling I could see him cough as the brushstroke strayed at odd angles, the unnatural gap between characters a pause for painful breath. Thousands suffered from Yokkaichi asthma in those days, and the constant exhale of the chemical factories hung as white clouds, settled over the city, and on windless days seemed to block the sun, Fukutomi's widow said. Even the fish in the bay came off the hook with warts and black spots along their spines, smelling like grease, tasting like gasoline, and they left a slick feeling on our tongues that sometimes took days to go away, but we ate them anyway, because we remembered how hungry we'd been, and we couldn't afford to throw them out.

 I started walking in the hope of dispelling the emptiness that fills me after a long period of work, and planned to walk the remains of the pilgrimage route to the Grand Shrine, which houses the sun deity Amaterasu, and if I had the time and felt physically capable, connect to the trails leading to the far side of the Kii Peninsula. The idea felt vaguely spiritual, and perhaps I thought I could regain something lost from too many hours at my desk. That first evening I stayed at the Konishi, just outside Tsu, and feeling the unseen gazes from shop windows and darkened homes, I couldn't prevent a rising anxiety as I walked alone on the gravelly sidewalks. When I visited Tsu years ago, pedestrians crowded the walkways and alleys, the buildings downtown rose defiantly, reflecting afternoon light in their sheer glass, shining down, casting everything an optimistic yellow, but now I found the city translucent, like watered-down ink, the few cars fleeing desperately through the streets. Across from the Konishi, a pudgy middle school student with straining uniform buttons glanced from side to side as he fed a thousand-yen note into an Asahi Beer vending machine. The inn's sliding door scratched and stuck against its paneling, the inside smelled of must and aging straw, and when I told the proprietor I had a reservation, he eyed me suspiciously, as if aware he needed my patronage, but not wanting a stranger to stay in his home, and he scrutinized a tattered sheet, the reverse printed with minutes from the Tsu Athletic Association's fall meeting, and just as the fear that he might turn me away tightened my breathing, he motioned to follow him, and disappeared down the dark hall. After depositing my bag in my cell and soaking in the Konishi's dim bath, I sat alone, cross-legged on the dining room tatami, waiting for the dinner that comes with a stay at Japanese inns. A naked bulb threw shadows across the room, accentuating the distance to the peeling walls, and a young woman of about thirty materialized with a tray, leaving the door open behind her. She bowed before serving my food, and as she leaned forward, the edge of her kimono collar hung open slightly, revealing a blotchy red pattern that crept from her collarbone along the back of her neck, and, seemingly horrified at the prospect that I might start a conversation, she gave another hasty bow and returned to the shadows. I spent a restless night turning on a futon worn so thin I could feel the seams between the tatami underneath me, my room's claustrophobic air crystallizing as feverish images of factory clouds and patchy walls, and the young woman's inflamed skin surfaced in my mind, the red on her neck spreading to her arms and beyond her fingers, out through the Konishi's floors and walls, spilling from my window into the morning sky that, when I finally opened my eyes, shone as streaks of pink and yellow, and after a breakfast of dry fish, miso soup, and rice, I shouldered my pack and continued south.

Beyond Tsu, the plains gave way to brief views of the water, and as the western mountains edged to the coast, I detoured to visit my friend Taro Iwaoka, curator of the Motoori Norinaga Memorial Museum in the ruins of Matsusaka Castle. The city center is dominated by the ruins—devoid of actual buildings, only the castle walls remain, stones rising twenty meters high with streets and homes spiderwebbing out in rough circles—the same way Tokyo sprawls from the Imperial Palace, or Beijing from the Forbidden City—and I was reminded I once read that we construct cities as reflections of our cosmology, that to understand a community's philosophy, one simply has to find the tallest structure. I paused to gaze up at the wall face, and as I stared at the rock pattern against the sky, lost the sense of whether I was looking up from the earth, or down at drifting clouds from some impossibly high place, and had to reach a hand out against the stone to steady myself. People come from all over the country to see these walls, they're quite famous for the way the stones are largely untreated, Taro later told me, construction commenced just before the civil war ended Japan's feudal period, and the daimyo at the time employed Hasegawa Seijuro, head of the Anoshu stonemasons, as architect. The Anoshu were elite craftsmen, but they had a reputation for being eccentric—Seijuro said he could hear the voices of stones—and his family survived five generations with no allegiances,

and the warring daimyo, constantly needing better defenses, continued to hire the Anoshu because, they are said to have said, everyone else was. Hasegawa Seijuro compiled the lessons from his family's work rising and falling over one hundred years, determined to use them in Matsusaka Castle. The idea, Seijuro said, Taro told me, was to make a fortress not only impervious to attack and livable under long periods of siege, but create an entirely natural structure, pleasing to the senses. While the masons cut the edges on some of the stones, they mostly fit them together without mortar or tools, and the cumulative effect is somewhat unnerving, and today, the unique construction makes the community unwilling to repair or refurbish, for fear that tourists will say the castle is no longer original, and stop coming. For his part, Hasegawa Seijuro was so obsessive in completing his vision, he bankrupted nearby quarries and, when construction still wasn't finished, he turned to graveyards—you can still find tombstones with names and dates built into the walls. Of course, the civil war ended before the castle did, and while it was considered the most technically impressive fortress at the time—impregnable, its daimyo declared, Taro told me—it never saw action; the samurai and administrative staff were stripped of their titles, and the castle towers left to rot. That same daimyo— Gamo Ujisato, young military prodigy of the Japanese west—was reassigned to lead the invasion of Korea, and died before he saw action, struck down by food poisoning in Kyoto before even starting his campaign, and I get the sense that the people of Matsusaka somehow enjoy the fact that they can say now, because of his untimely death, Ujisato's unrealized potential was limitless.

When I entered the museum lobby, Taro was waiting for me, and he greeted me with a half-bow, half-wave—thin hand rising and shabby hair falling—in a gesture I'd only ever seen him make to me. I visited Norinaga's residence recently for the first time in some weeks and, as I paused to look out his study window on the second story, in a bit of an indulgence I rang the little bell that still hangs on the windowsill, and noticed that the plum blossoms were finally starting to open. But with the photographer here last week and the NHK interview the week before, things have been so busy that I'm afraid I haven't made the progress I'd hoped with my annotations, Taro said, but please, he went on, guiding me with an open hand, I'd like to hear more about your trip. We entered his office, a rectangular room packed with books rising from chairs and tables to the ceiling— only a thin strip of bright hardwood led from the door to an open area with his desk and two cracking leather couches, and the rising books felt something like a hedge maze. As the bursting couch creaked under my weight, I had a strange sense of comfort, as if pausing for a moment of peace after navigating to the center of a labyrinth, and realized that since I'd known him, Taro always kept his offices like this, and while he made no effort to clean or organize, the papers and books also never seemed to grow or multiply—they simply sat in the same place, unopened and unused, yellowing with the passing months.

In the times that I'd visited the Motoori Norinaga Museum, and for the work it seemed that Taro was unceasingly engaged in, I can't remember ever seeing a single patron inside, and, as the museum receptionist slipped in wordlessly, placing a tray with two porcelain cups of black coffee and plastic-wrapped red bean mochi on the table between us, I wondered that her days must be filled sneaking glances at her phone, gazing out to watch the shadows of the castle walls lengthen to evening, waiting for the day to end so that she can lock the doors and wipe the exhibit cases when the museum closes at exactly 4:30 p.m. Before Taro was assigned as curator, Norinaga had been only a phantom in my mind, belonging to a past I couldn't quite place. He's a bit of a polarizing character, and it's surprising a city would invest the time and money to build a new museum dedicated to him, Taro said to me once, and I'm surprised Matsusaka would willingly bear the risk. At the time, when I expressed that I knew very little of Norinaga besides the museum's basic description of doctor by day, scholar by night, Taro betrayed an almost imperceptible look of shock, from which he quickly recovered, and leaned forward with a lowered voice. This city, it's obsessed with the idea of him. We highlight things we want to highlight, that his

home was on the pilgrimage route, that he and Ozu Yasujiro are part of the same family, and we accentuate certain details—like how he would shoulder a wooden case of drawers, a portable medical cabinet, common in those days, and make house calls throughout the town. Even though western medicine was growing in popularity, he refused to study anything not Japanese—his most famous case, you may know, was a young boy suffering from an unknown illness, unable to get out of bed. His mother tried the newest methods available but nothing worked, and after inquiring for a traditional doctor, she found Norinaga and asked him to come examine the child, and with the mother standing by looking onward with hands clasped at her chest in visible distress, Norinaga, noting the mother's show of emotion, diagnosed that she was the cause of the illness, and that the boy should be made to work. Of course, we discuss this anecdote when we're mentioning how insightful he was—after all, he could see the mother was spoiling the child, we say—but we don't talk about what happened to the family after. Regardless, he wasn't known for advancing medicine, but literature and aesthetics, and, as you know, worked constantly through the nights, and while the city refuses to mention it, some of his later diary entries led me to believe that he sacrificed his eyesight working by candlelight too much, and if you examine the few portraits of him, his eyes always seem unfocused and cataractous, but the city doesn't want to draw undue attention to any imperfections—rather, the most human thing we talk about is how when he grew tired he would stand at the window of his study on the second story of his house, and ring the bell that he kept there, that the sound would revive some great power within him, and he could continue his work, now tireless, far into the night.

But you're walking to the Grand Shrine, Taro said, reaching for his cup of coffee and leaning his elbows onto his thighs, and when I told him I'd reached a break in my work, he nodded, and we chatted about my research, and the annotations he'd been making on Norinaga's commentaries of the ancient Japanese classics. But let me show you what I'm working on, Taro said, suddenly rising from his couch and making his way through his narrow path of books. I followed him to the second floor of the museum, where he unlocked a conference room, the double doors revealing a spreading diorama of what was obviously the city of Matsusaka. The partially completed model was expansive, covering most of the conference room floor—to do any sort of work on it, one would ostensibly have to be sitting or kneeling on the ground— and although the miniature buildings were clearly meant to be constructed in the style of Japan's feudal era, the city didn't look all that different from how it did in the present, and it gave me the strange feeling that I was gazing down at our current location as one sometimes does in a dream. Although he was supposed to be annotating Norinaga's commentary of *The Tale of Genji*, Taro had been told the diorama takes priority, as the director was obsessed with giving guests something to make Norinaga's Matsusaka feel more alive. The director was insistent that they have historical precedent for every detail, and each business and home must be accurate to its place on the fifth lunar month

of 1763, when Norinaga began his work on the classics and discovered mono no aware. It was the director's idea to use this specific date, which, Taro told me, makes him feel the need to explain mono no aware to guests—I've heard the term described as the transience of things, but I've also heard it as the ahness of experience, the feeling you get when you're enjoying time with friends and family and have a sudden awareness that the moment will pass, or when you're viewing cherry blossoms in an early spring snowfall, and understand that with the slowly warming days, the cherry blossoms too will eventually fall. But when I read it, I think of it as a feeling of inevitable erosion, that even as our lives pass, our memories continue to move in some way, and while the images may blur and fade in our minds, the past continues to return to us.

When Taro walked me to the front of the museum and gave his bow-wave, the sun was already creeping to the mountains in the west and, judging I didn't have enough time to make it to the next town, I walked past the Korean barbeque restaurants and bars that line the road to the train station and, passing the giant statue of Norinaga's bell that has become a symbol of the town, found a business hotel I'd stayed at some years ago. I spent the evening eating tasteless soba and settling in my room to make notes on the walk so far, and set out early the following day, determined to reach the Ise Grand Shrine before afternoon. In the late morning, I paused to rest in the shadow of an empty mochi shop—the opposite side of the road opened to an early rice paddy, the green rising and spreading to the horizon—my pack scratched as I set it down against the concrete, the break in my steps now a sudden warmth in my legs, and I stood and watched the wind glittering silent through the field, the stillness giving slow movement to the clouds against the sky.

Most visitors to the Grand Shrine make their way by car or train—the nearest station drops them conveniently two blocks from the entrance of the shrine complex, forcing them through a gauntlet of gift shops and restaurants, constructed in dark wood and tile roofs made to look feudal, advertising local novelties identical to the items on sale in every other part of the country. On foot, however, I navigated the old road through a maze of deserted shopping malls and dilapidated shrines—entire city blocks seemingly abandoned when the new highway and train line were constructed—and after a wrong turn into a covered mall, found myself alone among shuttered shops, light streaming through gaps in the disintegrating metal roof that reminded me of photos I'd seen of flooding subterranean caverns, holes to the surface world and, with growing fatigue in my legs and blisters forming on the heels of my feet, began to feel a sense of hopelessness rising. Records suggest that the Ise Grand Shrine served millions of annual visitors during Japan's feudal period, and today, about eight million people make the trip every year. While I'd spent much of the previous three days walking alone in silence, the sudden crush of tourists, student groups, families, and couples was a stark contrast to the open areas I'd been through. One approaches the shrine's main gate by a massive stone staircase surrounded by ancient camphors, and I found the hundreds of people waiting on the steps scrolling through their phones somewhat undermined the holy aspect of the place. I read once, in a brochure about the Grand Shrine, that the sun goddess

Amaterasu chose this location because she found it quiet and peaceful, a suitable place to enshrine herself. I couldn't help feeling somewhat melancholy that a deity seeking quiet would find herself confronting eight million guests each year, crowding the roads and trains to the area. Amaterasu is the same deity, Taro once told me, that Norinaga himself spent a great deal of time researching. The fruit of his efforts, ultimately, was that he traced Amaterasu to the Imperial Family, using ancient records, thus proving the divinity of the emperor through holy texts. This, as you know, came to be known as the empirical evidence that justified the actions of the empire through the twentieth century and, Taro said, the museum and the Grand Shrine are more concerned with presenting something positive for tourists—it's simply easier not to mention that inconvenient aspect of Norinaga's history. I found myself exhausted after the visit to the Grand Shrine, perhaps from the three days of walking, perhaps from the sudden influx of people, and, after making my way to the southern outskirts of town, found the Suzuya Inn. After a quick bath, I succumbed to a hard sleep. The following morning, I continued south to Toba, walking along the entrance of the bay leading to the Pacific, the islands and coastline marked with dozens of abandoned resorts, hotels with busted windows towering over the water, memorials to the economic miracle of the eighties, left to rust and crumble when the bubble burst and the visitors stopped coming. As the coastline swung to the west, opening views of the ocean, I paused to pray at a tiny roadside shrine tilting violently with age and decay, refusing to fall as if held up by some lonely, stubborn god.

CONTRIBUTORS

Izidora Angel is a Bulgarian-born writer and literary translator. Her work has appeared in *Astra, Best Literary Translations 2024, Chicago Reader, Sublunary Editions, Words Without Borders,* and elsewhere. She has received recognition from the National Endowment for the Arts, English PEN, Art Omi, and the Elizabeth Kostova Foundation. She lives in Chicago.

Mateo Askaripour is the author of the novels *Black Buck* (Mariner), for which he was a National Book Foundation 5 Under 35 honoree, and *This Great Hemisphere* (Dutton). He lives in Brooklyn.

Anna Ballbona is a Spanish journalist and writer. She is the author of two novels in Catalan, *Joyce i les gallines* [Joyce and the Hens] and *No soc aquí* [I'm Not Here] (both Anagrama).

Anne P. Beatty's work has appeared in *The American Scholar, The Atlantic, New England Review,* and elsewhere. She lives in Greensboro, North Carolina, where she is a high school English teacher.

Yordanka Beleva is a Bulgarian writer and poet. She is the author of four poetry collections, most recently *Central Newscast*; and four story collections, most recently *Hedgehogs Come Out at Night*. In English, her stories have appeared in Izidora Angel's translation in *Best Literary Translations 2024, Two Lines,* and *Words Without Borders*.

Jack Boucher (1931-2012) was an American photographer for the National Park Service. He traveled through forty-nine states and two U.S. territories to photograph for the Historic American Buildings Survey, the Historic American Engineering Record, and Historic American Landscapes Survey.

Suzanne Buffam is the author of three collections of poetry, most recently *A Pillow Book* (Canarium). She lives in Chicago.

Nancy Naomi Carlson's translations include Khal Torabully's *Cargo Hold of Stars: Coolitude,* which received the Oxford-Weidenfeld Translation Prize, and, with Esperanza Hope Snyder, Wendy Guerra's *Delicates* (both Seagull). She is the author of three poetry collections, including *Piano in the Dark* (Seagull) and serves as the translations editor for *On the Seawall*.

Adam Clay teaches at the University of Southern Mississippi and edits *Mississippi Review*.

Megan Cummins is the author of the story collection *If the Body Allows It* (University of Nebraska) and the novel *Atomic Hearts,* forthcoming from Ballantine. She is the managing editor of *Public Books* and an editor at large at *A Public Space*.

Graham Foust's most recent book is *Terminations* (Flood Editions). He lives in Colorado, works at the University of Denver, and sometimes teaches in the MFA program at the University of Nebraska Omaha.

Calvin Gimpelevich is the author of *Invasions* (Instar), which was a finalist for the Lambda Literary Award in Transgender Fiction. His work has appeared in *The Best American Essays 2022* and been recognized by the Seattle Office of Arts & Culture, the Studios at MASS MoCA, the Kimmel Harding Nelson Center for the Arts, and elsewhere.

CJ Green was a 2023 Writing Fellow at A Public Space. An editor for several years at a theology journal, he received an MFA from the Iowa Writers' Workshop. His work has appeared in *Image, Prairie Schooner,* and *The Rumpus*. He lives outside Iowa City.

Kimiko Hahn's most recent poetry collection is *Foreign Bodies* (Norton). Her collaborations include the chapbook *Dovetail* with Tamiko Beyer; writing text for Bill Brand's experimental documentary *Coal Fields,* and writing poems for visual art projects, among them the art book *poetics* and photograph broadsides with Lauren Henkin. She teaches at Queens College, City University of New York.

Philippe Halsman (1906-1979) was born in Riga, Latvia, and began his photographic career in Paris, where he photographed many well-known artists and writers, including André Gide, Marc Chagall, Le Corbusier, and André Malraux. He arrived in the United States in 1940, and over the next thirty years his reportage and photography were featured in numerous American magazines, including 101 covers for *LIFE*. His *JUMP Book* includes portraits of 191 jumps by politicians, movie stars, authors, Nobel Prize laureates, athletes, theologians, and others he asked to jump for him.

Cory Howell Hamada was a 2023 Writing Fellow at A Public Space. He has worked in Japan as a coordinator for international relations and as the lead writer for *National Geographic's Expedition: Earth* podcast series, and his work has been published in *National Geographic Learning*. He lives in California.

Kirsten Kaschock is the author of five poetry books, most recently *Explain This Corpse* (Lynx House). and the novel *Sleight* (Coffee House).

Kate Kruimink is a writer from southern Tasmania. She is the author of the novels *Heartsease* (Picador Australia) and *A Treacherous Country* (Allen & Unwin), which received the Vogel/Australian's Literary Award. Her novella "Astraea," which appears in this issue, was one of three recipients of the inaugural Weatherglass Novella Prize from Weatherglass Books in England.

Rosemary Laing (1959-2024) was an Australian artist. She was honored at the 35th Higashikawa International Photography Festival in 2019, receiving the Overseas Photographer Award for photographic achievements.

Mike Lala is the author of *Exit Theater* (Colorado Prize for Poetry) and *The Unreal City* (Tupelo), and several chapbooks, including *Twenty-Four Exits: A Closet Drama* (Present Tense Pamphlets). His installations, performances, and libretti include *Whale Fall* and *Madeleines: Tell Me What It Was Like*.

Cildo Meireles is a Brazilian conceptual artist, installation artist, and sculptor.

Samira Negrouche was born in Algiers where she continues to live. She is the author of seven poetry collections, including *The Olive-Trees' Jazz and Other Poems* (Pleiades), which was translated by Marilyn Hacker and shortlisted for the Derek Walcott Prize for Poetry and the National Translation Award in Poetry. She is also the author of several artists' books and has participated in various multidisciplinary projects. The poem in this issue is the first section of *Traces*, a collaboration with choreographer Fatou Cissé loosely structured around the theme of movement, which is forthcoming from Seagull Books.

Ucheoma Onwutuebe received an MFA from the University of Nevada, Las Vegas. Her work has appeared in *Catapult, Passages North, Bellevue Literary Review*, and elsewhere. She has received residencies from Yaddo, Art Omi, and The Anderson Center. Her story in this issue was edited by Lydia Mathis as part of her 2023 Editorial Fellowship at A Public Space.

Naz Riahi's work has appeared in *Harper's Bazaar, Guernica, Los Angeles Review of Books, Food & Wine,* and *Pipe Wrench* among other publications. Her writing has been nominated for a James Beard Award.

James Shea is the author of *The Lost Novel* and *Star in the Eye* (both Fence Books), the co-translator of *Moving a Stone: Selected Poems of Yam Gong* (Zephyr), and the co-editor of *The Routledge Global Haiku Reader*.

Kate Shepherd has exhibited at museums and galleries across the United States and Europe since 1994. Her most recent museum solo exhibitions include *Kate Shepherd: Lineaments* at the Charlotte and Philip Hanes Art Gallery at Wake Forest University and *Intersections: Relation to and yet not (homage to Mondrian)* at the Phillips Collection in Washington, D.C.

Art Smith (1917-1982) was born in Cuba. From the mid-1940s until 1979, he crafted jewelry in his Greenwich Village studio and shop in New York City. His work was the subject of the posthumous exhibit *From the Village to Vogue* at the Brooklyn Museum in 2008.

Peter Trachtenberg is the author of three books of nonfiction. The piece in this issue is adapted from his fourth book, *The Twilight of Bohemia: Westbeth and the Last Artists in New York*, a history of America's first publicly funded artists' housing project, which is forthcoming from Godine.

Lawrence Venuti, professor emeritus

of English at Temple University, is a translator from Italian, French, and Catalan, as well as a translation theorist and historian. He is the author most recently of *Contra Instrumentalism: A Translation Polemic* (University of Nebraska), and the translator of *The Bewitched Bourgeois: Fifty Stories by Dino Buzzati,* which is forthcoming from New York Review Books.

Yee Heng Yeh is a writer and translator from Malaysia, and was a 2023 Writing Fellow with A Public Space. His work has been featured on the podcast *KITA!,* and published in *adda, Strange Horizons, Mantis,* and *Nashville Review.* He is the poetry editor for *NutMag,* a zine based in Penang.

CREDITS

IMAGES

Page 3: Cildo Meireles, *Insertions into Ideological Circuits: Coca-Cola Project,* 1970. Tate, presented by the artist 2006, accessioned 2007. © Cildo Meireles.

10: Jack Boucher, *View of house between two casinos,* Town of Atlantic City, North end of Absecon Island, South of Absecon Channel, Atlantic City, Atlantic County, NJ, 1933. From the Historic American Buildings Survey.

14, 15: Art Smith, jewelry. Courtesy Mark McDonald and the Estate of Art Smith.

42, 43, 94, 95: Kate Shepherd, *Selfie*, 2017. Enamel on panel. *Helena Lights*, 2018. Screen print and enamel on panel. *Eavesdropper,* 2019. Enamel on panel. *Earth*, 2019. Enamel on panel. All ©Kate Shepherd. Courtesy Galerie Lelong & Co.

124-125: Rosemary Laing, *Flight Research #6.* ©The Estate of Rosemary Laing. Courtesy Galerie Lelong & Co.

152, 153 209: Philippe Halsman *Thomas E. Dewey, Governor of New York,* 1965. American actress Kim Novak. Dick Clark at Philippe Halsman's studio, *1958.* All ©Philippe Halsman / Magnum Photos. Permission of Magnum Photos.

TEXT

150: "Lockdown Drill" was selected by Rebecca Makkai as the winner of the Academy for Teachers' 2024 Stories Out of School Flash Fiction Contest.

PATRONS

BENEFACTORS
Anonymous
The Hawthornden Foundation
Drue & H. J. Heinz Charitable Trust
Yiyun and Dapeng Li Baiteng Zhao

SUSTAINERS
The Chisholm Foundation
Google, Inc.

PATRONS
Anonymous
Katherine Bell
Daniel Handler and Lisa Brown
Charles and Jen Buice
Rimjhim Dey
Deb Dowling
Brigid Hughes
Siobhan Hughes
Binnie Kirshenbaum
Lisa Lubasch
Elizabeth McCracken
John Neeleman
Paul Vidich and Linda Stein
Margo and Anthony Viscusi

SUPPORTERS
Stacy Blain
Patricia Hughes and Colin Brady
Jamel Brinkley
William Buice
Christopher Carroll
Matthea Harvey and Robert Casper
Sarah Chalfant
Annie Coggan and Caleb Crawford
Megan Cummins
Nicole Dewey
Dow Jones & Company, Inc.
Jennifer Egan
Elizabeth Gaffney
Michael Gerard
Tracie Golding
Elizabeth Howard
Dallas Hudgens
Padraig and Vanessa Hughes
Cressida Leyshon
Mike Lindgren
Diane T. Masucci
E.J. McAdams
Fiona McCrae
Diane Mehta
Honor Moore
Michael Moore
Garth Greenwell & Luis Muñoz
The New York Review of Books
Jonathan Sapers
Brett Fletcher Lauer and Gretchen Scott
Margaret Shorr
Robert and Suzanne Sullivan
Emily Tarr
Brian Tart
Leon Trainor
Deborah Treisman
Mengmeng Wang
The Whiting Foundation
Chris and Antoine Wilson
Renee Zuckerbrot

SUPER FRIENDS
Julia Ballerini
Susan Davidoff
Tom Fontana
Mary Stewart Hammond
Elliott Holt
Mary-Beth Hughes
Jodi and John Kim
Joan Kreiss
Miranda and Jorge Madrazo
John Neeleman
Ed Park
Sarah Blakley-Cartwright and Nicolas Party
Chen Reis
Josh Rozner
Kelly Sather
Finley Shaw
Pavel Shibayev
Ira Silverberg
Sam Swope
Nafeesa Syeed
Joan Wicks
Heather Wolf
Peter von Ziegesar

FRIENDS
Karen Ackland
Claire Adam
Margaret Weekes and Frederick Allen
Sasha Anawalt
Lisa Almeda Sumner
Susan Alstedt
Julia Anderson
Sam Ankerson
Anonymous (8)
Lili Arkin
Christine Back
Shahanara Basar
Margaret Beal
Aimee Bender
Paul Beckman
Eve Begiarian
Dana Bell
Carly Berwick
Kaethe Bierbach
Robert and Ann Brady
Jennifer Braun
Nicholas Bredie
E Phoebe Bright
Jamel Brinkley
Lisa Brody
Claudia Brown
Suzanne Buffam
Kimberly Burns
Katherine Carter
Sara Miller Catterall
Louise Chadez
Padmasini Chakravarthy
Lucian Childs
Sunny Chung
Patricia Clark
Patty Cleary
Jane Ciabattari
Christen Diane Clifford
Federica Cocco
Bruce Cohen
Nancy Cohen
Gerard Coleman
Martha Cooley
Craig Literary
Irene Cullen
Lynne Cummins
Larry Dark
Nancy Darnall
Chelsea DeLorme
Lawrence Desautels
Kerry Dolan
Judith Dollenmayer
Sheryl Douglas
Vicki Madden and Jim Ebersole
Brian T. Edwards
Paula Ely
Pamela Erens
FabStitches LLC
Barbara Faulkner
Michael Faulkner
Teresa Finn
William Finnerty
Kathryn Fitch
Nancy Ford Darnall
Katharine Freeman
Peter Friedman
Carrie Frye
Reginald Gibbons
Molly Giles
Jane Glendinning
James Goodman
Richard Gorelick
Jonathan Grant
Mark Gross
Jaclyn Green-Stock
Roger Greenwald
Barrie Grenell
Margaret Griffin
Ron Griswold
Christine Fischer Guy & Andrew Guy
Jessica Haley

Philippe Halsman, *JUMP (Dick Clark)*

PATRONS

Karen Hall
Thomas Hanzel
Christine Happel
Maria Harber
Deborah Harris
C.E. Harrison
Melissa Havilan
Diane Heinze
Joshua Henkin
Claudia Herr
HOLSEM
Sarah Jane Horton
Randal Houle
Marilyn Hubert
Samantha Hunt
Mary Iglehart
Yuxue Jin
Raymond Johnson
Tom Johnson
David Wystan Owen & Ellen Kamoe
T Maya Kanwal
Daphne Klein and Zach Kaplan
Vivien Bittencourt and Vincent Katz
Heather Kelly
Jessie Kelly
Joshua Kendall
Kirpal Khalsa
Kristin Keegan
Theresa Kelleher
Jena H. Kim
Nancy Klein
Eileen B Kohan
Kimberly Kremer
Glenn Kurtz
Joan L'Heureux
Laura Lampton Scott
Carol Lappi
Nancy Lawing
Vivian and Alan Lawsky
Barbara Lawson
Jeffrey Lependorf
Mark Lewis
Jing Li
Don Liamini
John Lillich
Annie Liontas
Long Day Press LLC

William Love
Graham Luce
Katherine Mackinnon
Gregory Maher
Jeremy Martin
Nancy J. Martinek
Robert McAnulty
Julia McDaniel
Elizabeth and McKay McFadden
Claire Messud
Jennifer R. Miller
Rachel Buckwalter Miller
William Morris
Judy Mowrey
Lubna Najar
Maud Newton
Elizabeth Norman
Idra Novey
Cliona O'Farrelly
Beth O'Halloran
Mo Ogrodnik
Eric Oliver
Zulma Ortiz-Fuentes
George Ow, Jr.
Danai M Paleogianni
Sandra Park
Carolie Parker
Sigrid Pauen
Perlita Payne
Sunny Payson
Samuel Perkins
Mary Perushek
Debra Pirrello
Sarah Gay Plimpton
Kathryn Pritchett
Yan Pu
Kirstin Valdez Quade
Alice Quinn
Jon Quinn
Carlos Ramos
Chicu Reddy
Tina Reich
Adeena Reitberger
Mickey Revenaugh
Ann Ritchie
Susan Z. Ritz
Sarah A. Rosen
Julia Rubin

Nicole Rudick
Ruth and Kirsten Saxton
Peter Schmader
Jill Schoolman
Fern Schroeder
Wayne Scott
Jennifer Sears-Pigliucci
Diana Senechal
Elizabeth Shepardson
Brian and Melissa Sherman
Nedra Shumway
Murray Silverstein
Tina Simcich
Judy Sims
Gabrielle Howard and Martin Skoble
Michele Smart
Adrianna Smith
Karen Smith
The Smith Family
Timothy Soldani
Sarah Soliman
Maria Soto
Peter Specker
Laura Spence-Ash
Helen Wickes and Donald Stang
Judith Sturges
Kevin Thurston
Elizabeth Trawick
Rick Trushel
Brooke Tucker
Georgia Tucker
Charity Turner
Marina Vaysberg
Franklin Wagner
Terry Wall
Patricia Wallace
Marcia Watkins
Joyce Watts
Meg Weekes
Susan Wheeler
Katie Wilson
Mary Beth Witherup
Sierra Yit
Jenny Xie
Diane Zorich

"A CABINET OF WONDERS"*

GERTRUDE ABERCROMBIE
HUSSAIN AHMED
LAYLAH ALI
JAMES ALLEN HALL
SELVA ALMADA
JJ AMAWORO WILSON
KAREN AN-HWEI LEE
RUSSELL ATKINS
MARY JO BANG
ARI BANIAS
BRUCE BARBER
MEGAN BERKOBIEN
MARK BIBBINS
KAYLA BLATCHLEY
DANIEL BORZUTZKY
MARCEL BROODTHAERS
LILY BROWN
DAVID BOYD
ANNE BOYER
JAMEL BRINKLEY
NIN BRUDERMANN
PETER BUSH
BRIAN CALVIN
LEA CARPENTER
WENDY CHEN
ANNIE COGGAN
KATE COLBY
MARGARET JULL COSTA
GREGORY CREWDSON
P. SCOTT CUNNINGHAM
BRUNA DANTAS LOBATO
KIKI DELANCEY
MÓNICA DE LA TORRE
YOHANCA DELGADO
JILL DESIMINI
JENN DÍAZ
ALEX DIMITROV
TIMOTHY DONNELLY
ANNE ELLIOTT
EMMET ELLIOTT
INDYA FINCH
GRAHAM FOUST
JOHN FREEMAN
WILL FRYER
MINDY FULLILOVE
ELISA GABBERT
CHLOE GARCIA ROBERTS
N. C. GERMANACOS
TEOLINDA GERSÃO
REGINALD GIBBONS
MARIA GILISSEN
CASSANDRA GILLIG
KRISTEN GLEASON
MICHAEL GOLDBERG
MATTHIAS GÖRITZ
MARZIA GRILLO
MARILYN HACKER
MARK HAGE
SARAH HALL
DAVID HAYDEN
STEFANIA HEIM
JAMIL HELLU
JORDAN JOY HEWSON
HILDA HILST
MISHA HOEKSTRA
JENNY HOLZER
BETTE HOWLAND
TIMOTHY HURSLEY
ARINZE IFEAKANDU
RANA ISSA
LÍDIA JORGE
FADY JOUDAH
ALEXANDER KAN
KRISTIN KEEGAN
JENA H. KIM
ROBERT KIRKBRIDE
TAISIA KITAISKAIA
JAMIL KOCHAI
SANA KRASIKOV
JHUMPA LAHIRI
EDUARDO LALO
DAVID LARSEN
AMY LEACH
LE CORBUSIER
SUZANNE JILL LEVINE
YIYUN LI
KELLY LINK
GORDON LISH
ARVID LOGAN
BEN LOORY
MARIE LORENZ
BRIDGET LOWE
VICKI MADDEN
JORDANA MAISIE
NIKKI MALOOF
KNOX MARTIN
RANIA MATAR
MELISSA MCGRAW
PHOEBE MCILWAIN BRIGHT
MEREDITH MCKINNEY
DEIRDRE MCNAMER
JAMES ALAN MCPHERSON
ALEXANDER MCQUEEN
EDWARD MCWHINNEY
CLAIRE MESSUD
CLEO MIKUTTA
STEVEN MILLHAUSER
GOTHATAONE MOENG
QUIM MONZÓ
INGE MORATH
SUNEELA MUBAYI
TAWANDA MULALU
BONNIE NADZAM
DORTHE NORS
CATHERINE PIERCE
TAYLOR PLIMPTON
ANZHELINA POLONSKAYA
ALISON POWELL
JULIA POWERS
LI QINGZHAO
ANNA RABINOWITZ
PACO RABANNE
NATASHA RANDALL
NEAL RANTOUL
SRIKANTH REDDY
RICHARD ROBBINS
MERCÈ RODOREDA
MATTHEW ROHRER
SAMUEL RUTTER
SASHA SABEN CALLAGHAN
CHERYL SAVAGEAU
SALVATORE SCIBONA
DENISE SCOTT BROWN
SCOTT SHANAHAN
AL-SHAMMAKH IBN DIRAR
FARIS AL-SHIDYAQ
CALLIE SISKEL
MAHREEN SOHAIL
EVA SPEER
THOMAS STRUTH
ROBERT SULLIVAN
CLAIRE SYLVESTER SMITH
FIONA SZE-LORRAIN
DEBORAH TAFFA
ZSUZSA TAKÁCS
KAT THACKRAY
ERNEST THOMPSON
SYLVAN THOMSON
COLM TÓIBÍN
RICHARD TUTTLE
NANOS VALAORITIS
CORINNA VALLIANATOS
THANASSIS VALTINOS
MIYÓ VESTRINI
LATOYA WATKINS
KYLE FRANCIS WILLIAMS
MINDY WONG
JENNY XIE

*Whiting Literary Magazine Prize

SUBSCRIBE TO A PUBLIC SPACE

A PUBLIC SPACE BOOKS

A TERMINATION
Honor Moore

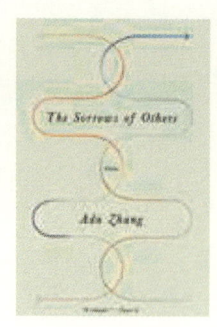

THE SORROWS OF OTHERS
Ada Zhang

GOD'S CHILDREN ARE LITTLE BROKEN THINGS
Arinze Ifeakandu

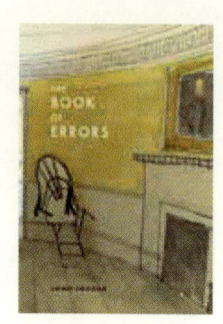

THE BOOK OF ERRORS
Annie Coggan

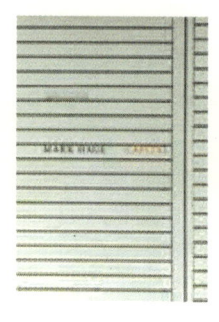

CAPITAL
Mark Hage

THE COMMUNICATING VESSELS
Friederike Mayröcker

GEOMETRY OF SHADOWS
Giorgio de Chirico

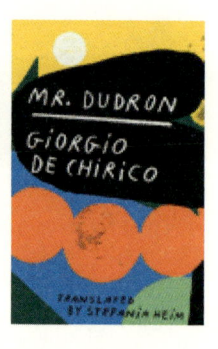

MR. DUDRON
Giorgio de Chirico

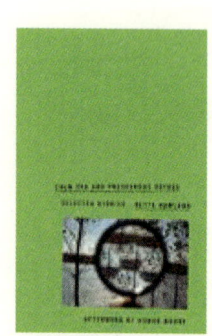

CALM SEA AND PROSPEROUS VOYAGE
Bette Howland

W-3
Bette Howland

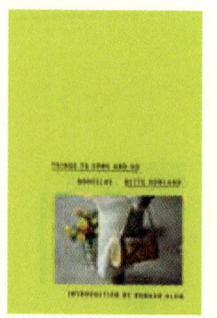

THINGS TO COME AND GO
Bette Howland

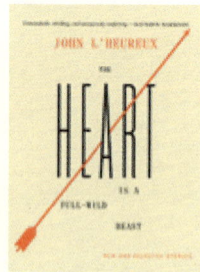

THE HEART IS A FULL-WILD BEAST
John L'Heureux